The
Internet

OPPOSING VIEWPOINTS®

Other Books of Related Interest

The Internet

OPPOSING VIEWPOINTS®

Helen Cothran, *Book Editor*

Daniel Leone, *Publisher*

Bonnie Szumski, *Editorial Director*

Scott Barbour, *Managing Editor*

OPPOSING
VIEWPOINTS®
SERIES

Greenhaven Press, Inc., San Diego, California

10/01

45757859

Cover photo: Photodisc

Library of Congress Cataloging-in-Publication Data

The Internet / Helen Cothran, book editor.
   p. cm. — (Opposing viewpoints)
   Includes bibliographical references and index.
   ISBN 0-7377-0779-8 (pbk. : alk. paper) —
ISBN 0-7377-0780-1 (lib. : alk. paper)
   1. Internet—Social aspects. 2. Internet—Social aspects—
United States. I. Cothran, Helen. II. Series

HM851 .I57 2002
303.48'34—dc21
                                       2001018761
                                            CIP

Greenhaven Press, Inc., P.O. Box 289009
San Diego, CA 92198-9009

"Congress shall make no law. . .abridging the freedom of speech, or of the press."

First Amendment to the U.S. Constitution

The basic foundation of our democracy is the First Amendment guarantee of freedom of expression. The Opposing Viewpoints Series is dedicated to the concept of this basic freedom and the idea that it is more important to practice it than to enshrine it.

Contents

Why Consider Opposing Viewpoints?

"The only way in which a human being can make some approach to knowing the whole of a subject is by hearing what can be said about it by persons of every variety of opinion and studying all modes in which it can be looked at by every character of mind. No wise man ever acquired his wisdom in any mode but this."

John Stuart Mill

In our media-intensive culture it is not difficult to find differing opinions. Thousands of newspapers and magazines and dozens of radio and television talk shows resound with differing points of view. The difficulty lies in deciding which opinion to agree with and which "experts" seem the most credible. The more inundated we become with differing opinions and claims, the more essential it is to hone critical reading and thinking skills to evaluate these ideas. Opposing Viewpoints books address this problem directly by presenting stimulating debates that can be used to enhance and teach these skills. The varied opinions contained in each book examine many different aspects of a single issue. While examining these conveniently edited opposing views, readers can develop critical thinking skills such as the ability to compare and contrast authors' credibility, facts, argumentation styles, use of persuasive techniques, and other stylistic tools. In short, the Opposing Viewpoints Series is an ideal way to attain the higher-level thinking and reading skills so essential in a culture of diverse and contradictory opinions.

In addition to providing a tool for critical thinking, Opposing Viewpoints books challenge readers to question their own strongly held opinions and assumptions. Most people form their opinions on the basis of upbringing, peer pressure, and personal, cultural, or professional bias. By reading carefully balanced opposing views, readers must directly confront new ideas as well as the opinions of those with whom they disagree. This is not to simplistically argue that everyone who reads opposing views will—or should—change his or her opinion. Instead, the series enhances readers' understanding of their own views by encouraging confrontation with opposing ideas. Careful examination of others' views can lead to the readers' understanding of the logical inconsistencies in their own opinions, perspective on why they hold an opinion, and the consideration of the possibility that their opinion requires further evaluation.

Evaluating Other Opinions

To ensure that this type of examination occurs, Opposing Viewpoints books present all types of opinions. Prominent spokespeople on different sides of each issue as well as well-known professionals from many disciplines challenge the reader. An additional goal of the series is to provide a forum for other, less known, or even unpopular viewpoints. The opinion of an ordinary person who has had to make the decision to cut off life support from a terminally ill relative, for example, may be just as valuable and provide just as much insight as a medical ethicist's professional opinion. The editors have two additional purposes in including these less known views. One, the editors encourage readers to respect others' opinions—even when not enhanced by professional credibility. It is only by reading or listening to and objectively evaluating others' ideas that one can determine whether they are worthy of consideration. Two, the inclusion of such viewpoints encourages the important critical thinking skill of objectively evaluating an author's credentials and bias. This evaluation will illuminate an author's reasons for taking a particular stance on an issue and will aid in readers' evaluation of the author's ideas.

It is our hope that these books will give readers a deeper understanding of the issues debated and an appreciation of the complexity of even seemingly simple issues when good and honest people disagree. This awareness is particularly important in a democratic society such as ours in which people enter into public debate to determine the common good. Those with whom one disagrees should not be regarded as enemies but rather as people whose views deserve careful examination and may shed light on one's own.

Thomas Jefferson once said that "difference of opinion leads to inquiry, and inquiry to truth." Jefferson, a broadly educated man, argued that "if a nation expects to be ignorant and free . . . it expects what never was and never will be." As individuals and as a nation, it is imperative that we consider the opinions of others and examine them with skill and discernment. The Opposing Viewpoints Series is intended to help readers achieve this goal.

David L. Bender and Bruno Leone,
Founders

Greenhaven Press anthologies primarily consist of previously published material taken from a variety of sources, including periodicals, books, scholarly journals, newspapers, government documents, and position papers from private and public organizations. These original sources are often edited for length and to ensure their accessibility for a young adult audience. The anthology editors also change the original titles of these works in order to clearly present the main thesis of each viewpoint and to explicitly indicate the opinion presented in the viewpoint. These alterations are made in consideration of both the reading and comprehension levels of a young adult audience. Every effort is made to ensure that Greenhaven Press accurately reflects the original intent of the authors included in this anthology.

Introduction

"The Net's impact—the widespread availability of two-way electronic communications—will change all of our lives."

—*Esther Dyson, futurist and author of* Release 2.0

When television became popular in the 1950s, it provided a window to the world, but it also encouraged people to spend less time outside visiting with neighbors. The automobile furnished people with mobility, but it also created pollution and led to the creation of suburban sprawl. Today, the Internet allows people to access unlimited amounts of information and connect with people around the world, but some experts believe it has also led to social isolation and loss of privacy. As David Mennahum and a group of eleven other technology writers assert, "Technology is making life more convenient and enjoyable, and many of us healthier, wealthier and wiser. But it is also affecting work, family, and the economy in unpredictable ways, introducing new forms of tension and distraction, and posing new threats to the cohesion of our physical communities." The Internet has already precipitated far-reaching social and economic changes, yet in its present form, the Net is just over ten years old.

The Internet seemed to appear suddenly in the early 1990s, but its development really began twenty years earlier. In 1969, the Pentagon's Advanced Research Projects Agency (ARPA) was asked to create a communications network that would survive a nuclear attack. The research team linked four university computers in a network—called ARPAnet—so that if one of the computers in the network was destroyed, the other three could continue to exchange data. ARPAnet was utilized primarily by engineers and scientists.

ARPAnet continued to attract the interest of academicians, but—since it required complex commands to operate—it was difficult to use. In an effort to make a computer network that would be easier to operate, computer experts continued to explore different protocols—the computer standards that enable different computers to communicate with one another.

The protocol Unix—developed in 1978—made newsgroups possible for the first time. Newsgroups allow users to talk with one another about their favorite topics over a network. BITNET (Because It's Time Network) connected IBM mainframe computers and was eventually linked with the burgeoning Internet, which allowed for the exchange of e-mail, now the most widely used part of the Net.

With the advent of new Internet protocols, networks became progressively easier to use. However, as more universities and organizations began to post information on the Internet, it became increasingly difficult to navigate. In response, tools to index Internet resources were developed. The first user-friendly Internet interface—Gopher—was developed in 1991 and is still used today. Gopher allows people using personal computers to download information from universal servers, the model for today's Internet.

However, Gopher is a text-based interface that many users still find formidable. A more slowly developed, but ultimately more popular protocol was a graphics-based distribution standard proposed by the European Particle Physics Laboratory in 1989. This graphics-based protocol—based on hypertext, which allows users to follow links to other documents— eventually became the World Wide Web (WWW). In 1993, the Web browser Mosaic was introduced by Marc Andreessen, who later helped design the Netscape Navigator Web browser, which, along with Microsoft's Internet Explorer, helped popularize the Web. Browsers allow users with no knowledge of complex Internet protocols to use the Internet with ease. The popularity of the Web has also provided an incentive for commercial interests to create their own websites, which has led to an explosion in Internet commerce.

From its modest beginning as a network linking four university computers, the Internet has grown to an international network of more than forty thousand computer networks accommodating more than fifty million users. Indeed, Morgan Stanley Technology Research reports that the Internet is the world's fastest-growing communications medium in history. It took thirty-eight years for radio to reach 50 million homes in the United States and thirteen years for television to do so. In contrast, many experts claim that the Internet has exceeded that level of penetration in just ten years. According to a survey conducted by the Pew Research Center for the People and the Press, 49 percent of U.S. residents were Internet users in 1999, a 30 percent increase from 1996. Average Internet users spend around seven hours per week surfing the Net, time they used to spend watching television, talking on the phone, and reading, according to the *Los Angeles Times*.

The rapid growth of the Internet has resulted in profound social and economic changes. Those who see the Internet as a positive technology claim that it has helped people become enlightened, enabled individuals to voice diverse opinions, built relationships between people, and bolstered the economy. Paul Gilster, author of *Digital Literacy*, claims that the Internet has "inherent power in creating connections between people and institutions where before there were none." On the other hand, critics of the Internet claim that the technology has isolated people, provided an avenue for pornography pushers to ply their trade, fostered hate and terrorism, and become a tool of the elite. Internet critic Clifford Stoll, author of *Silicon Snake Oil*, writes, "What good does it do our society to take us away from a close, physical community and put us in touch with distant strangers? The things people yearn for most—a community, a relationship with commitment and trust—are exactly what you don't have online."

Technologies such as the automobile, the telephone, and the Internet often effect unforeseen changes. The Internet, because it has grown so quickly, especially exemplifies the paradoxical nature of technology. To be sure, technology is not neutral—it affects society, for good and for ill—and history eventually records both the negative and positive impacts of each new technology. The authors in *The Internet: Opposing Viewpoints* debate some of the most contentious issues concerning the Internet in the following chapters: How Does the Internet Affect Society? How Will the Internet Affect American Institutions? Should the Internet Be Regulated? What Will Be the Future of the Internet? As Internet technology evolves from a four-computer network to a wireless medium connecting millions of people worldwide, it will continue to shape society in the future.

CHAPTER 1

How Does the Internet Affect Society?

Chapter Preface

Many psychiatrists believe that people who spend too much time on the Internet can become "cyberjunkies," users who are addicted to online shopping, gambling, computer games, or sex. These pastimes can entice Internet users into spending more and more time online, away from their responsibilities.

Many experts claim that the most common Internet addiction is to pornography. According to Brian McCormick, writer for the *American Medical News*, there are more than 2 million Internet sex addicts. Internet sex addicts compulsively visit pornographic websites and spend copious amounts of time in chat rooms engaging in sexually explicit conversations. David N. Greenfield, a psychologist specializing in Internet addiction, argues that Internet addiction can result in "increased social isolation and withdrawal, a possible increase in depression, family separation, marital problems, and reduced job performance." Some commentators maintain that addiction to Internet sex harms society because it can lead to sexual dysfunction such as pedophilia.

However, not all experts believe that a preoccupation with Internet sex can be classified as an addiction. The American Psychiatric Association has yet to include sexual addiction in its diagnostic manual, for example. Even if Internet sexual compulsivity could be called an addiction, many analysts simply don't believe that the problem is widespread enough to be considered a serious threat to society. Richard Goldstein, reporting for the *Village Voice*, explains that "most people who surf for sex—between 83 and 99 percent in the best-known study—don't get hooked." Many commentators point out that sexual deviance such as pedophilia existed long before the Internet's popularity.

Internet addiction—to gambling, shopping, or sex—is just one of the potential social impacts of the Internet currently under debate. Observers wonder whether the Internet creates problems or is merely being blamed for problems that already exist. The authors in the following chapter discuss what effect the Internet has on society.

> "The problem isn't the Internet. The suburbs and the long automobile commutes to our workplaces have fragmented our lives and perhaps left us too far apart."

The Internet Can Help People Stay Connected

Janna Malamud Smith

Janna Malamud Smith is a clinical social worker and author of the book *Private Matters: In Defense of the Personal Life*. She argues in the following viewpoint that the Internet is blamed for social problems that existed long before the Internet was invented. She asserts that the Internet actually makes it easier for people to connect with one another in a society where suburban sprawl has fragmented communities. In addition, Smith maintains that people are attracted to the Internet because it allows them to interact with others while still enjoying privacy and solitude.

As you read, consider the following questions:
1. What personal example does Smith use to illustrate why human contact is not always preferable to interaction over the Internet?
2. Why does the author think that using the Internet is preferable to watching television?
3. Why do people move apart when given the chance, according to Smith?

The Internet is a member of our family. According to my monthly bill, each of us spent about 5.4 hours a week online, which makes us pretty much average American Net users. I can't speak for the rest of my family, but I relish my online time. A new study tells me that I should feel bad about that. Bourbon, red meat, whole milk and the Internet, too?

Human Contact: A Mixed Bag

According to the 2000 study, by Norman Nie, a political scientist at Stanford University, the Web makes us even lonelier and more isolated than we already are. "The more hours people use the Internet, the less time they spend with real human beings," Professor Nie said. There is a danger, he claimed, of worsening social isolation and creating a deadened and atomized world without human emotion.

Could that be possible? Or are we perhaps confusing the bandage with the wound? For starters, it seems that Professor Nie is assuming that hours with real human beings are an unqualified good thing. Call me a curmudgeon, but I often find them to be something of a mixed bag.

Did I miss fighting the shopping mall crowds at Christmas to buy one of my sons a hat he had really wanted? Not at all. Spending 15 minutes online as opposed to two hours (minimum) searching for parking, then trudging from store to store to have indifferent teenage clerks shrug their shoulders and mutter, "No problem," is not a human contact I crave.

The days when a trip to the milliner's meant a nice exchange with a friendly proprietor you've known for years are long gone in my neighborhood. On the other hand, thanks to Net shopping I was able to buy my husband a beautiful bow tie made by hand by a woman in Maine.

Staying Connected

Online in the last couple of weeks of February 2000, I've kept in touch with busy friends, some of whom live halfway around the world, and tracked temperatures in Seville, Spain, which we are visiting next month. I've easily located and purchased out-of-print books from small secondhand dealers and looked up some useful exercises for a knee I had hurt.

Each of these little solitary outings made me shamefully

happy. In fact, learning that it was 65 degrees in Seville when it was 10 above zero and icy in Massachusetts was the single most mood-elevating discovery I made in the first two weeks of February.

Driving to work this week, I listened to callers on a radio talk show discuss a novel about transsexuals. Several callers who identified themselves as transsexuals talked about how much comfort and communion they'd felt from visiting certain Web sites just for them. You can't tell me that this is worse than spending endless hours interacting with the real people around them who may think they are nuts. While "atomizing" culture can be a problem, it can also allow more diverse stories to emerge and so reduce the silent suffering of the tellers.

Online Romance

Anyone who doesn't have a date for Valentine's Day just isn't plugged in. Literally. With more than 1,200 dating sites operating on the World Wide Web, someone to toast the most romantic of holidays with could be just a few mouse clicks away.

Dating sites, which are more precise, interactive versions of personal ads, are the fastest-growing way for single people to meet other eligible adults. They have made such an impact on the singles market that more traditional competitors like the video dating service Great Expectations are giving members an online option.

Trolling the Web for new romantic candidates is becoming so common that it is fast losing its image as the last resort of leftovers and weirdos.

Mimi Avins, *Los Angeles Times*, February 13, 2000.

When I came home tonight, my 14-year-old son was ecstatic because he had finally gotten access to the chat room his school friends visit. Rather than sitting in front of the television to unwind after his homework was done, he happily chatted with his buddies. Yes, it would be better if all his friends lived on the same block so they could all hang out together in person. But connecting online may be the best alternative.

People already spend a lot of time alone, even when they are with their families. I've heard many parents with multiple televisions in their homes talk about how everyone scatters after supper to watch a separate program.

According to the Stanford report, of the people in the study who are online five or more hours a week (about 20 percent of those surveyed), 59 percent are spending less time watching television. Is that making life worse? Online, some of the conversations are two-way.

I grant that there are concerns. My husband, who teaches at a boarding school, told me about an interesting faculty discussion about the pros and cons of wiring each dormitory room for Internet access. Would it help the students, or pull them away from their studies and their friends?

I recently told my 14-year-old that he couldn't put his computer in his bedroom and had to keep it in the family room. I didn't explain that I had made that decision because I wanted to keep an eye on what he was downloading, nag him when he has spent too much time online and pat his head occasionally, but I think he guessed. Yes, we all need to monitor this powerful tool.

Society and Solitude

When people gain more money and more choices, it seems they often choose to move farther apart. Out of the one-room tenement, out of the bed shared with siblings, off the subway.

Why? Part of the answer is that privacy and solitude are very attractive and often emotionally salubrious states. People enjoy being unobserved and left in peace—some of the time. And I think "some of the time" is the vital point that's being lost. Privacy and solitude, even anonymity, feel wonderful when they are chosen. When they're imposed, they tend to feel awful. Then they mutate into isolation, loneliness, depression and anomie, and Prozac sales skyrocket.

But the problem isn't the Internet. The suburbs and the long automobile commutes to our workplaces have fragmented our lives and perhaps left us too far apart. And, yes, some people are too isolated and lonely. (Though I hold that in the past, many people were made equally miserable by too much forced contact.)

So I suggest that we turn some attention to helping people find pleasurable ways to get back together. And helping them make time to do it. Even transcendentalist writer Ralph Waldo Emerson recommended "Society and Solitude."

To prosper emotionally, people need to feel wanted, needed and valued. Our failure to offer this prospect to many citizens long precedes the World Wide Web. And making sensational and premature proclamations about the Internet's harm simply distracts us from addressing those social conditions that drive us apart. Let's not go for the virtual damage when the real thing is before us.

> *"Cyberspace opens new doors for the kind of racial acrimony that acts like an acid upon our efforts to establish a harmonious multiracial community."*

The Internet Does Not Build Meaningful Connections Between People

Douglas Groothuis

In the following viewpoint, Douglas Groothuis contends that the Internet does not provide the trust and human interaction necessary to build community. He asserts that the anonymous nature of Internet speech encourages deceit and hate speech. Furthermore, Groothuis maintains that not everyone has the economic resources to buy the new technology or the expertise to use it. Douglas Groothuis is assistant professor of philosophy of religion and ethics at Denver Seminary and author of the book *The Soul in Cyberspace*, from which this article is adapted.

As you read, consider the following questions:
1. What pranks does Groothuis describe in order to illustrate that the Internet is conducive to deception?
2. According to the author, why does the adage "seeing is believing" not apply to the Internet?
3. What are "media viruses," according to the author?

A now famous cartoon in the *New Yorker* shows one dog saying to another, "On the Internet, nobody knows you're a dog." In his bestselling cheer for everything digital, *The Road Ahead*, Bill Gates exults that "anyone can send anyone else a message on the Internet," and notes that correspondents "who might be uncomfortable talking to each other in person have forged bonds across a network." (Gates laments that the incorporation of video technology with e-mail and other forms of communication on the Net, while much to be desired in some respects, will "do away with the social, racial, gender, and species blindness that text-only exchanges permit.")

The Exclusive Cyberspace Community

Gates's comments are curious. First, it is not true that "anyone can send anyone else a message on the Internet." This is true for Gates and his friends, to be sure, but most people are still strangers to cyberspace, either because they don't have the stamina to master a new and often intimidating technology or because they simply do not have the financial resources to connect. As of now, users of the Internet are overwhelmingly young, while, middle to upper-middle class, and male—although the extent of women's involvement seems to be increasing fairly rapidly. Connections of various kinds are being made through cyberspace, but these electronic rendezvous do not seem to be crossing gender, class, and racial barriers in any significant way. Many worry that the juggernaut of advancing cyberspace technologies will leave economically disadvantaged people out of the information loop.

Even if computers become more affordable for more people, how will poorer folks learn how to use them, especially if schools in lower-income neighborhoods have less access to computer education? As computer expert and cyberspace critic Clifford Stoll has pointed out, the cyberspace community is not as friendly as it often claims to be. Because of the "exclusionary nature of technocratic culture," it is up to the user to figure out which system is best, to decipher the new, jargon-heavy terminology and to install and maintain the software. Outsiders are often put off by "a liturgy of technology."

The Problem of Anonymity

Second, the anonymity of nonvideo interaction in cyberspace is a two-edged sword. On the one hand, textual communication can be a leveler. On screen, a person is judged only by his or her words. It is reasonable to imagine that people who might otherwise avoid each other would willingly converse through e-mail. If the impersonal medium enhances the personal dimension instead of eclipsing it, these online relationships could be converted into more full-blooded off-screen encounters. On the other hand, I am afraid this pleasant scenario requires a basic honesty and integrity that the culture of cyberspace often lacks. Furthermore, the particularities of race, age, gender, and economic status cannot forever be erased if people are to know each other as embodied beings in the physical world. A racist may converse online with someone of another race, whom he comes to appreciate as being a good writer, well educated, and friendly. The crunch comes, though, when the racist finds that his e-mail correspondent is typing with hands of another color. If the racial anonymity is never broken, no progress toward racial reconciliation can be forged. If racial realities are revealed and prejudice continues, nothing has changed.

The same problems exist for age, gender, and economic status. What kind of community is being created when its members are digitally sheared of these characteristics? Community worthy of the name is largely fashioned out of the recognition of our embodied and sometimes awkward particularities, within a context of regarding one another as fellow humans worthy of respect and civility. The Christian deepens this by adding that people are made in the image and likeness of God; they are not only our neighbors, they are objects of divine concern. Civil communities—places where a soul may flourish with other souls—ask its to present ourselves as we truly are before others as they truly are, that we might learn where we agree, where we disagree, how to disagree agreeably, and how to assist and persuade each other through compassion and reason.

Community Requires Trust

Community is impossible without some level of trust, even among strangers. We try to live in a good neighborhood where we can trust those around us not to accost us or harm our property. We must trust our accountants and our medical doctors to be reasonably competent with our assets and our bodies. How much can cyberspace reinforce trust? Francis Fukuyama puts a damper on cyberspace optimists, such as Albert Gore, Alvin and Heidi Toffler, George Gilder, and Newt Gingrich, who think that computer technologies will decentralize knowledge, eliminate hierarchies of all sorts, and liberate the masses from political oppression. He points out that trust is indispensable for cultural and economic betterment, and that it is not easily established through the largely impersonal interaction of computer technologies. Fukuyama writes in *Trust: The Social Virtues and the Creation of Prosperity* that "trust does not reside in integrated circuits or fiber optic cables. Although it involves an exchange of information, trust is not reducible to information." Rather, "trust is the expectation that arises within a community of regular, honest, and cooperative behavior, based on commonly shared norms . . . of other members of that community." Developing this kind of behavior when cyberspace is our primary means of interaction is difficult if not impossible. Virtual communities are often just too virtual to trade on this kind of trust. In many ways, the nature of cyberspace is conducive to deception. The day after the Oklahoma City bombing,[1] a message was posted in the Usenet database (misc.activism.militia), which read:

> OK City bombed by FBI. Now they begin their black campaign in order to spread as much terror as possible. . . . They will try to tie it to Waco. Janet Reno is behind this, the campaign will succeed because the media will persuade the public. Expect a crackdown. Bury your guns and use the codes.

The San Francisco Chronicle, USA Today, Newsday, the *Atlanta Journal-Constitution*, and other newspapers referred to this message with great alarm at the frightening prospects it evoked. Its author, however, was not a wild-eyed extremist but a journalism student at the University of Montana who posted the message as a joke. Similar pranks have involved

---

1. On April 19, 1995, the Murrah Federal Building in Oklahoma City was bombed, killing 168 people. In 1997, Timothy McVeigh and Terry Nichols—both connected with the militia movement—were convicted in connection with the bombing.

claims about alien autopsies, Microsoft buying the Vatican, the dreaded modem tax, and phony political Web pages.

Clifford Stoll mentions watching an online interview with California governor Pete Wilson. Evidently a poor typist, Wilson barely answered five questions. There was little opportunity for compelling political discourse. Stoll observes, "Seeing his text intermittently scroll across my screen, I realized that I had no way of knowing if [Wilson] himself was at the keyboard or merely one of his minions."

Seeing Is No Longer Believing

The old adage "seeing is believing" is now itself unbelievable, at least with respect to many electronic media. The digital darkening of O.J. Simpson's[2] face on the cover of *Time* magazine is a case in point. No one would have known the difference if *Newsweek* had not run the same mug shot without the alteration. This type of digital manipulation can be perpetrated in cyberspace as well, and may never be exposed. In *Scientific American*, photography expert William J. Mitchell observes that "we are approaching the point at which most of the images that we see in our daily lives, and that form our understanding of the world, will have been digitally recorded, transmitted and processed." Altered photos were far more easily discerned before digital manipulations became available. Today, "digital images are manipulated by altering pixel values stored in computer memory rather than by mechanically altering surfaces." This process hides the alterations quite nicely, as several illustrations in Mitchell's article make clear. Photographic evidence—whether on screen or in print—is no longer above suspicion. This adds new poignancy to Jesus' admonition that we not judge merely according to appearance, but with sober judgment. Yet the necessity of such constant suspicion in cyberspace hardly builds trusting communities.

Media Viruses

As a medium, cyberspace is peculiarly amenable to the spread of what Generation-X guru Douglas Rushkoff calls "media viruses": ideas that infect the masses at rapid speeds and in

2. O.J. Simpson—once a football hero—was acquitted in 1995 of murdering his ex-wife, Nicole Brown Simpson, and her friend, Ronald Goldman.

Online Personalities Incompatible with Offline Realities

Internet enthusiasts point out (correctly) that duplicity and manipulation have been enduring facts of human history and that the advent of computer-mediated communication raises at most questions of degree rather than kind. I must confess that I come away unconvinced. Considerable evidence suggests that the Internet facilitates the invention of online personalities at odds with offline realities and that the ability to simulate identities is one of its most attractive features for many users (gender-bending is said to be especially popular). But the playful exercise of the imagination, whatever its intrinsic merits and charms, is not readily compatible with the development of meaningful affective [emotional] ties.

William A. Galston, *Philosophy & Public Policy*, Fall 1999.

---

novel ways through electronic media. The Net makes possible a dissemination of ideas that bypasses the traditional intermediaries of editorial control, paper publishing, material transport, and so on. Of course, this can be used for good or ill; but cyberspace presents the opportunity for particularly virulent ideas to pollute people's minds in unprecedented ways.

Emerge magazine recently ran an exposé of racist groups who are exploiting the Net with evangelistic determination. Various white supremacist cadres—neo-Nazis, skinheads, identity groups, and others—are employing sophisticated technologies to proselytize. The Net allows these clandestine groups to network with each other as never before. A number of civil rights groups, such as the Klanwatch Project of the Southern Poverty Law Center, are attempting to monitor such groups. In April of 1996, a skinhead group disseminated a photograph of a prone black man being kicked by a white person. Another hate-mongering group advocates taking advantage of cyberspace anonymity to post injurious messages that appear to be written by "the enemy" (African Americans). They also advise other despicable racist practices. One white supremacist declares that "cyber-guerrillas" should "grasp the weapon which is the Net, and wield it skillfully."

Although such irrational prejudice has been alive since sin entered the world, cyberspace opens new doors for the kind of racial acrimony that acts like an acid upon our efforts to establish a harmonious multiracial community. Unless there is a concerted and courageous stand for racial equality and reconciliation, the burning cross may shoot out sparks that spread like wildfire in the corrupted sectors of cyberspace. . . .

Generally speaking, the kind of community required for the resuscitation of national life requires the grace that comes through the human touch, the human voice, the human gaze. Genuine community shines through the human presence of truth expressed personally. Cyberspace can only mimic or mirror these experiences (however convincingly); it cannot create them. It can, however, beguile us into mistaking connectivity for community, data for wisdom, efficiency for excellence, and virtual democracy for an informed and active citizenry. It can even beguile us into worshiping the works that our hands have made. If cyberspace is kept closely fastened to the real world, and if we refuse its temptations to replace the literal with the virtual, it can in some ways enhance the natural bonds of humans in society. If not, it may instead eclipse much of what is good and true in genuine community.

*"The digital divide is not an abstract idea
but a matter of economic viability, political
equality and education opportunity."*

Unequal Access to the Internet
Harms Society

Anthony G. Wilhelm

Anthony G. Wilhelm contends in the following viewpoint
that not all Americans have access to the Internet, nor will
market forces enable them to connect to it in the near future. He claims that the poor, the elderly, ethnic minorities,
and those living in rural areas lag far behind affluent Americans in their ability to purchase and use computer technology. This gap—called the "digital divide"—prevents many
adults from participating in online elections, and it bars their
children from learning skills needed to compete for high-
paying jobs. Anthony G. Wilhelm is director of the Communications Policy Program at the Benton Foundation and
author of the book *Democracy in the Digital Age*.

As your read, consider the following questions:
1. How much more likely are households with an income of
   $75,000 to have Internet access than those at the lowest
   income levels, according to the author?
2. According to Wilhelm, by what percentage do white
   households outnumber African-American and Hispanic
   households online?
3. How many towns with a population of ten thousand or
   fewer have cable-modem service, according to the author?

The digital divide is one of those policy issues—global warming is another—that is fobbed off by a coterie of decisionmakers with the pretense that the problem is more illusory than real. The argument regarding Internet diffusion usually goes: If we are at the beginning or middle along the adoption curve, then the question really is not whether households will come online, but how long it will take until the market serves everybody. Those who believe that the digital divide is just a shibboleth suggest that the issue is more about "have-nows" vs. "have-laters" than about an enduring information underclass. With price points coming down and Internet service being given away, the public is taking to the Internet like children to Pokémon. So what's the problem?

Have-Nows Versus Have-Laters?

Let's step back for a minute and define terms before we give shape to the problem. The digital divide usually is described as the unequal access to computers and the Internet that breaks along familiar socioeconomic fault lines, such as income, education, race and age. Those groups on the wrong side of the divide often are called the technology have-nots and include a disproportionate share of people living in poverty, functional illiterates, American Indians, blacks living in the South, people in small rural towns and people older than 60.

Detractors who claim that the issue is about have-nows vs. have-laters make a leap of faith: that the market will serve everybody in short order. They ignore penetration lags that will shut out whole communities and groups from the benefits of Internet exchange, possibly through the better part of this decade and beyond. The problem, then, is less about how long it will take before the gaps close but rather what the likely impact is of excluding millions of Americans from the major artery of information, communication and commerce. Don't the detrimental effects of "e-exclusion" merit some sort of public response?

Excluding a disproportionate number of poor, rural, minority and older Americans from the online world is a major policy challenge. It is a threat to our democracy when cer-

31

tain groups cannot participate in online voting or express their preferences—thumbs up or thumbs down—on the growing list of political and civic Websites. This hypothesis was put to the test in Arizona in March 2000 when those registered voters who had remote Internet access were given the opportunity to vote online in the Democratic Party primary during the 96-hour period leading up to the opening of the polls, whereas those without access to the Internet were able to exercise their franchise for just one day at the polling place. How fair is this? No doubt this example of digital democracy is only the tip of the iceberg.

Uneven participation in online voting is only one example of how the digital divide has an adverse impact on our society in unacceptable ways. Students without access to the Internet at home and in school do not develop the skills to compete for the 1.3 million high-skill, information-technology, or IT, jobs that will open up during the next six years, not to mention the litany of occupations that require some familiarity with information technology. Thus, communities suffer from having unfilled jobs and an underskilled pool of potential employees. Households that are not online, moreover—particularly those in poverty—cannot benefit from job opportunities, social-service information and lifelong learning opportunities that build the capacity of all Americans. In short, lag time experienced by those not online can be lethal.

While computers and Internet service are becoming as ubiquitous as televisions in high-income households, this is a far cry from acknowledging that diffusion patterns now resemble a random cross section of America's population. As with other technologies, there is a saturation of upper- and middle-class adopters and a protracted time period ensues in which adoption rates for poor households increase incrementally. With the telephone, for example, it took 83 years after its invention in order for penetration to approach universal adoption, and significant gaps remain along income, ethnic and geographic lines.

Poverty and the Internet

Even the most optimistic market research suggests that low-income Americans continue to be hard to reach and are coming onto the Internet at rates much lower than middle-class Americans. The gaps between bottom and top economic quartiles in Internet access are yawning, and they persist over time. One study from the marketing firm Jupiter Communications showed that by 2005 at least one-half of all households earning less than $15,000 still will be unconnected. A study of Internet users by the U.S. Department of Commerce, *Falling Through the Net*, found that households with incomes of $75,000 and higher are more than 20 times more likely to have access to the Internet than those at the lowest income level.

Poverty not only affects the Internet use habits of adults and householders, but children as well. According to a re-

Connections

Plans to make Internet access as available as telephone service have a long way to go. Wide gaps exist between Internet haves and have-nots.

U.S. Households Using Telephones, Computers and the Internet

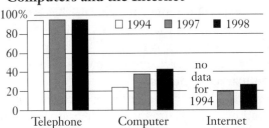

U.S. Households Using the Internet, by Race, Ethnicity and Income

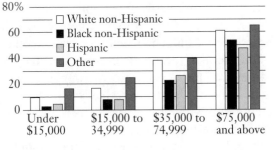

U.S. Department of Commerce, *New York Times*, January 27, 2000.

port from the Kaiser Family Foundation, only 23 percent of low-income kids have access to the Internet at home, compared to 58 percent of kids in high-income neighborhoods. In high-poverty neighborhood schools, moreover, students are much less likely to have instructional rooms connected to the Internet than are kids in more affluent, suburban communities, according to the U.S. Department of Education. Can we expect the market alone to serve the technology needs of schools with run-down facilities and sporadic access to 21st-century learning tools? Probably not—which is why the "e-rate" at the federal level has been critical, plowing close to $6 billion into poorer schools and libraries to discount the cost of telecommunications services.

The Internet Is Too Expensive

If we do not believe the research and data—that income explains in large measure the makeup of the Internet population—then let's listen to the attitudes of people as revealed in market surveys. Particularly for the poorest households, one-third say that the Internet is too expensive and, for those who experience Internet churn, the primary reason given for dropping off the network is the cost of service. In short, the poorest American adults, excluding students, remain the hardest to serve and the most immune to government and market solutions.

Of course, there are alternative delivery mechanisms coming online, such as interactive television and many computer and Internet giveaways. If computers and Internet service are falling off the back of trucks, then why should we assume that the problem will remain? First, the new delivery platforms, such as interactive television, are convenient, but they still cost money. A monthly charge usually is added to the Internet-service bill, and when this is added on top of cable fees and the like, these bills become too steep for many low-income customers. The free giveaways are vital, but the majority of these offers involve rebates (and consumers still need to come up with the up-front cash) and limited-time offers for free Internet service.

If we thought that poverty was a difficult enough problem to tackle, it is not the only hurdle in the way of universal ac-

Computers Are Beyond Reach of the Third World

There are about 5 billion people on Earth today. Only 150 million of them have access to computers—only 30 in every 1,000 or 3 percent. By comparison, 1.3 billion people on the planet live in absolute poverty—about 260 in every 1,000 without even a basic survival diet.

The way the system has *distributed* computers makes access even more unequal: the computers are *overwhelmingly* concentrated in a handful of the wealthiest imperialist countries, especially the U.S.

The U.S. alone, with only 5 percent of the world's people, has half of the world's computer capacity. Three-quarters of the world's phone lines are concentrated in the imperialist countries, where only 15 percent of the world's population lives.

For vast, vast stretches of this planet there are essentially no computers. Those that show up are overwhelmingly concentrated in the hands of various military forces or the offices of imperialist corporations. A quarter of the world's countries have more than 100 people for every working phone. In fact, about half of the people in the world have never even used a telephone!

In short, in oppressed Third World countries that contain the overwhelming majority of humanity, computers are beyond the reach of all but the most wealthy. And even for the wealthy, there is often no regular electrical current or stable connections to the global telephone networks that tie the Internet together.

Mike Ely, *Revolutionary Worker*, June 16, 1996.

cess to the Internet. Those people who have not completed high school make up only a tiny fraction of Internet users. Between 1997 and 1998 the divide between those at the highest and lowest education levels increased 25 percent, according to *Falling Through the Net*. An even thornier problem is the 44 million Americans who will not be able to navigate a text-based medium. Thus the digital divide is about more than plugging people into the Net. Antecedent resource gaps must be addressed that prevent millions of residents from going online.

The Rand Corp., a nonpartisan think tank, has shown that race and ethnicity also are barriers that show up as independent variables in research even when income and education are held constant. That study by Jupiter Communications, done in June 2000, showed that 60 percent more white households are online than African-American and Hispanic households, and a sizable gap will remain through 2005. American Indians are among the least likely groups to have Internet access—with a dismal 8 percent of rural Indian households having online access from home.

Another group unlikely to be online is those people who are older than age 60. According to one study, only 24 percent of Americans older than 60 have used the Internet or sent e-mail at home. In California, 67 percent of adults age 18 to 64 use the Internet compared to 27 percent of those age 65 and older, according to a study from the nonpartisan Public Policy Institute of California.

Rural communities also experience debilitating lag times. We know that the most important determinant of infrastructure deployment in rural areas is economic, with the cost of service increasing the more scattered the distribution of customers is. Only 5 percent of towns with a population of 10,000 or less have cable-modem service, compared to 65 percent of all cities with populations of more than 250,000. The issue of high-speed broadband delivery is a critical policy issue today and one that decisionmakers must address head-on to avoid broadband becoming the next-generation digital divide.

Ultimately our collective response to the digital divide hinges on our answer to two questions: Is there an enduring divide, one that market forces alone will not combat? And, if so, is it such a high-salience policy issue that it warrants sustained public and private support until the problem is resolved?

If there is equivocation on the first question, then clearly policymakers will take a wait-and-see approach, marginalizing the digital divide to a matter of diffusion curves and the laws of microprocessor speed. If there is acceptance of the first question but hedging on the second, then the issue is eclipsed by more immediate and fundamental concerns, such as fixing America's schools, ensuring health coverage for all or enacting campaign-finance reform.

Leadership remains fundamental and should be framed as a

matter of leveraging existing public and private-sector investments, as well as tying the discourse of the digital divide to everyday issues of common concern. The digital divide is not an abstract idea but a matter of economic viability, political equality and educational opportunity. Policymakers need to continue to step up and use their bully pulpit to advance the public-interest goals of equity and inclusion in the digital age.

"[Out-of-wedlock childbearing] is what shuts off poor children from American prosperity. Some sort of stable home life is what they need more than access to the Web."

The Problem of Unequal Access to the Internet Is Exaggerated

Eric Cohen

In the following viewpoint, Eric Cohen contends that civil rights leaders have exaggerated the problem of unequal access to computers and the Internet because they do not want to address deeper social issues such as out-of-wedlock childbearing that keep people poor. He claims that civil rights leaders use outdated studies to prove that such a digital divide exists. Moreover, Cohen insists that civil rights leaders ignore more current studies showing that minorities are actually purchasing computers more rapidly than Caucasians, which means that the digital divide is closing. Eric Cohen is managing editor of the *Public Interest* magazine.

As you read, consider the following questions:
1. According to Cohen, in the period from 1994 to 1998, what was the rise in the percentage of Caucasians who owned computers as compared to the percentage of African-Americans who did?
2. What factors have contributed to more African-Americans accessing the Internet, according to Ekaterina Walsh?
3. What percentage of married couples own computers compared to female-headed households, according to the author?

The "new new thing" in civil rights politics is just the latest variation on an old civil rights theme, the problem of inclusion—or, in digital divide-speak, the problem of access. The argument is familiar: Blacks and Latinos (unlike Asians) have, on average, lower incomes than whites because they have been ignored by the old-boy networks, shut out of the capital markets, and excluded from the well-financed elite schools that make white people so wealthy. Institutional racism is still the norm, and new technologies only promise to exacerbate old divides. It's "technological segregation," says National Association for the Advancement of Colored People (NAACP) president Kweisi Mfume; "apartheid," says civil rights leader Jesse Jackson. "Don't throw us aside, / close the digital divide," say the protesters in Silicon Valley [California, where the information technology industry is flourishing].

Falling Through the Net

The bible for this movement is a 1999 Commerce Department study—"Falling Through the Net: Defining the Digital Divide"—that activists cite with the agility of Talmudic scholars. "Whites are 2.5 times more likely to have home Internet access than Blacks and Latinos"; "the gap between whites and blacks grew by 53.3 percent between 1997 and 1998"; "more than a third of white families earning between $15,000 and $35,000 per year own computers, but only one-fifth of blacks do"—for reasons, President Clinton claims, that "we don't entirely understand."

There are other interesting statistics in the report: Asians at every income level are more likely than whites to own a computer; two-parent families of all ethnic groups are twice as likely to have Internet access as single-parent families (four times as likely among African-Americans). But these statistics are not cited with the same frequency or alarm as the official statistics on the race gap. "There just aren't the advocacy groups in place for single-parents," says Anthony Wilhelm, director of communications policy at the Benton Foundation, perhaps the key player in the digital divide movement and a major beneficiary of Internet service provider America Online's (AOL) multimillion-dollar largesse.

On the subject of race, the official statistics tell an ambiguous story. The major piece of evidence for Commerce Secretary William M. Daley's "racial ravine" is the following: Between 1994 and 1998, the gap between white computer ownership and black computer ownership grew from 16.8 to 23.4 percentage points. Sounds terrible. But read past the executive summary, and you discover the following: In 1994, 27.1 percent of white households and 10.3 percent of black households had computers. In 1998, the comparable figures were 46.6 percent for white households and 23.2 percent for blacks. Some basic arithmetic—conspicuously missing from the Commerce Department study, which presents the data in the most "alarming" possible way—shows that from 1994 to 1998, white ownership of computers rose 72 percent, black ownership rose 125 percent. In 1994, whites were 2.6 times as likely as blacks to own computers; in 1998, they were only twice as likely. The divide is not yawning wider; it's closing.

The Digital Melting Pot

This trend is consistent with another major study of Internet access—"The Digital Melting Pot," published by Forrester Research—which found that African Americans are getting home Internet access at a faster rate than any other ethnic group. Ekaterina Walsh, author of the Forrester study, projects that 40 percent of black households will be online at some point in 2000, while 44 percent of whites will—hardly a "racial ravine." Walsh gives three reasons for this: the rapid decline of computer prices; the increasing availability of free Internet access; and the surge of first-time computer buying during the 1998 and 1999 Christmas shopping seasons—periods not included in the Commerce Department study, which collected its data in December 1998. In Internet Time (computers are penetrating the marketplace seven times faster than electric service did and five times faster than telephones), December 1998 is another era. Even Larry Irving, former head of the National Telecommunications and Information Administration and the driving force behind the Commerce study, concedes that "we did miss a certain amount of information with regard to lower-priced PCs."

The Commerce study also exaggerated the "widening gap

between technology haves and have-nots" by excluding computers outside the home—in the workplace, in schools and libraries—from its many white vs. black comparisons. Indeed, in its 1998 report, which is the basis for its many "alarming" comparisons, the Commerce Department did not even collect data on out-of-home access. Digital divide advocates skillfully blur the issue to their political advantage: If it weren't for E-Rate (the Clinton-Gore program that uses new federal phone taxes to connect rural and inner-city schools to the Internet), they say, the digital divide would be worse. If government didn't step in, the racial ravine would be a racial abyss. But in their speeches, Clinton-Gore officials continue to use the Commerce Department figures that exclude school and work access—which is where most Americans, African Americans included, actually use the Internet.

A Cottage Industry

As much as a crusade, closing the digital divide has become a cottage industry for many Washington-New York-Silicon Valley intellectuals, civil rights leaders, and philanthropy bureaucrats. The Rainbow/PUSH Coalition, the National Urban League, the NAACP, and the Leadership Conference on Civil Rights have all called the digital divide the "new frontier of the civil rights movement." The Commerce Department has created a digital divide clearinghouse—digitaldivide.gov—to monitor the nation's progress. Nine major corporations (AOL, AT&T, Bell Atlantic, BellSouth, Gateway, Intel, iVillage, Microsoft, SBC Communications), the Ford Foundation, and the National Urban League have partnered with the Benton Foundation to create the Digital Divide Network (DDN), a clearinghouse "to enable and facilitate the sharing of ideas, information and creative solutions."

But apparently not all ideas are worth sharing. Andy Carvin, senior associate at the Benton Foundation and editor of the DDN, told me that "the website is absolutely comprehensive." But the Forrester report and other critical articles—such as those by David Boaz of the Cato Institute and Adam Clayton Powell of the Freedom Forum—are nowhere to be found. Anthony Wilhelm, communications policy director at the Benton Foundation, says of the Forrester report and others that criticize the concept of a digital divide, "the values these reports promote are not appropriate for a democratic society."

Dispersion of Technology Has Always Been Unequal

While it is true that the spread of the Internet has not been perfectly uniform, there is nothing unusual or inherently unfair about the way services are being delivered. As was the case with almost all previous technological innovations, the pace and pattern of the dispersion of technological advances to Main Street and Home Town America has never been perfectly uniform. New products and services have always been sensitive to income levels, demographics, and geography. Televisions, radios, and videocassette recorders started as luxury items within the reach of only a handful of Americans. Today, almost everyone has these products in their homes.

Adam D. Thierer, Heritage Foundation Executive Memorandum, February 1, 2000.

B. Keith Fulton, director of technology programs at the National Urban League, is similarly dismissive: "The Forrester study was based on 1,500, maybe 2,500 people polled by telephone. A lot of poor people, maybe 20 to 30 percent, don't even have phones. The Commerce Department study went door-to-door to 48,000 people. Now who are you going to trust? Methodology becomes important here." Maybe so, but the Forrester report was in fact based on a mail survey of 85,000 people.

Fact vs. Fiction

Not that either study is without weaknesses, but Forrester's numbers and projections are certainly more current and closer to reality than the Clinton administration's claims of a widening "racial ravine." You get the feeling, though, that the digital divide movement has already moved well beyond the need to be grounded in fact. It's now grounded in the need to perpetuate a winning issue. If there is no divide, there is no movement, so there must be a divide. Or, as Wilhelm puts it, "The [Benton] Foundation's identity has become closely connected to the digital divide and other equity issues."

In fact, the Commerce Department study has some very interesting findings—two in particular—that are either not discussed or not effectively explained. The first is that blacks and whites with incomes over $75,000 per year own computers and use the Internet at roughly the same rate, while low-income whites are almost twice as likely to own PCs as low-income blacks. Second, the divergence between single-parent and two-parent households is striking: 61.8 percent of married couples with children own computers, while only 31.7 percent of female-headed households do. Dual-parent white families are twice as likely to have Internet access as single-parent white families; dual-parent black families are four times as likely to have Internet access as single-parent black families. An obvious reason, besides income, suggests itself: Men are more often early adopters of technology than women.

The Key Is Income and Marriage

Altogether, the evidence suggests something like this: The economic boom of the last few years has made the vast majority of American families more wealthy; it has created millions of new high-paying jobs, especially in technology industries. As with white families, this has raised the incomes of millions of upwardly mobile black families, who now have enough money—and the desire—to buy computers. But there is a portion of the black community—a significant minority—that is not only chronically poor but burdened by unsafe streets, gang violence, and utter hopelessness. This group, not surprisingly, is not surfing the Web.

The key factor, as usual, is not race but income and marriage. In 1997, 69.2 percent of black children were born out of wedlock. This is the great tragedy that political leaders and captains of the computer industry who are philanthropically minded should be talking about. This—far more than "technological segregation" or "apartheid" corporate boards—is what shuts off poor children from American prosperity. Some sort of stable home life is what they need more than access to the Web. Which is, of course, the other great unsubstantiated claim of the digital divide movement: that what children especially need to succeed is more time in front of a computer. Skepticism about this claim actually grows the more one is familiar with how kids actually use computer access.

Couched in pro-market language and the hyperbole of the Internet age, the effort to close the digital divide is the latest version of the Jesse Jackson approach to social policy: talk about anything except the real cultural crisis of the under-class. To be sure, some of the digital divide efforts will have some positive effect—especially those dedicated to real men-torship rather than just computers in the classroom and tech-nology courses for teachers. There are no doubt worse things big government and corporate America could be spending money on. But, on balance, this latest crusade—the "fourth movement in the civil rights symphony," Jackson calls it—is based more on myth than reality, and offers only mythical solutions to real problems.

> *"Hatred has gotten a facelift. With the help of Internet technology and cyberspace marketing, once-decrepit organizations like the Ku Klux Klan are regaining their youthful energy."*

The Internet Fosters Hate Speech

Stacia Brown

Stacia Brown argues in the following viewpoint that hate groups are flourishing on the Internet because in cyberspace such groups enjoy anonymity and near-exemption from prosecution. Moreover, she claims that the Internet allows racists and other hate groups to disseminate their hateful messages more efficiently than in the past. Brown points out that hate groups use several tactics to make their views attractive, including using the Bible to justify racism. Stacia Brown works for the Emory University Center for Ethics in Public Policy and the Professions.

As you read, consider the following questions:

1. How many Internet hate groups does HateWatch monitor, according to Brown?
2. According to the author, what group of people do Christian fundamentalist hate groups tend to target?
3. What is the best way to make hate marketable, according to Brown?

Reprinted from "Virtual Hate," by Stacia Brown, *Sojourners*, September/October 2000, with permission from *Sojourners* magazine: (800) 714-7474; www.sojo.net.

Hatred has gotten a facelift. With the help of Internet technology and cyberspace marketing, once-decrepit organizations like the Ku Klux Klan (KKK) are regaining their youthful energy and competing for the attention of increasingly educated audiences. But don't let the good looks fool you: Behind the virtual makeover hides the same old-fashioned hatred that bigots have always promoted.

The Internet has given hate groups ample reason to feel young again. In the United States, online bigots enjoy full protection under the First Amendment and have access to a potentially limitless audience. Webmasters are anonymous and difficult to silence; leaders suffer few consequences for their followers' actions. And their strategies for organizational growth are beginning to look more corporate than cross-lit.

"The Internet has allowed hate groups to develop by leaps and bounds," states Dr. David Blumenthal, author of *The Banality of Good and Evil*. "The danger is that the uninitiated can get to them [hate sites]: people who are on the borderline and have been in the closet and now feel they can come out." Instead of leaflets under your windshield or on the lawn, haters now post their messages on the Web for you to find—by accident or choice.

Although America's free speech laws make prosecution of Internet haters difficult, their cyber-romps do not go unmonitored. Leaders in the anti-hate movement—including the Southern Poverty Law Center, the Simon Wiesenthal Center, the Anti-Defamation League (ADL), and HateWatch—are working to unmask cyber-bigots and expose their strategies to the public eye.

Who Are the Virtual Haters?

Brian Marcus has his work cut out for him. As research director for HateWatch, a five-year-old organization that tracks the movements of online haters, Marcus faces the task of identifying, categorizing, and monitoring between 300 and 350 Internet hate groups. HateWatch provides an exhaustive index of cyber-haters, covering everything from neo-Nazi to anti-Muslim to anti-disability groups. And while not all claim religious affiliation, an increasing number of groups—including anti-Christian, Christian and Racial Identity, and Christian fundamentalists—alternately attack, twist, or espouse the teachings of Christianity.

'For a Whiter World'

I have two daughters, a 6-year-old and a 3-month-old. I home school my oldest. I am a homemaker—when I did work I was an Office Manager and I also waited tables for a while. I have been a member of the World Church of the Creator (WCOTC) for two years and a Racial activist for eight years.

—Melody LaRue, Webmaster,
Sisterhood of the World Church of the Creator

On first read, Melody LaRue sounds like a fresh-faced evangelical with all the zeal of a mega-church devotee. She writes eagerly about her church and its efforts to bring new converts into the fold. Yet she is also a fiercely dedicated white supremacist, signing her e-mails "For a Whiter World, Sister Melody LaRue." The 25-year-old Seattle resident designs the women's Web pages for the World Church of the Creator, perhaps the best example of an anti-Christian religious hate group.

One of the largest and most active white supremacist groups in the United States, the WCOTC embraces religious structure and dogma but remains vehemently—even violently—opposed to Christianity. LaRue explains:

The WCOTC is definitely not a Christian church. In fact, we are anti-Christian. We believe that christ-insanity is one of the reasons that the White Race is in the position that it is in today. The "holy" bible teaches our people suicidal advice, such as "love your enemies. . . ." We have an extreme love for our people and refuse to follow teachings that will inevitably betray us.

Apparently LaRue's efforts are paying off. "There were over a thousand hits the first month," she says. "I am sure our new and improved Web site will get at least that much attention."

Using the Bible to Justify Hate

We believe in an existing being known as the Devil or Satan and called the Serpent (Genesis 3:1, Revelation 12:9), who has a literal 'seed' or posterity in the earth (Genesis 3:15) commonly called

(Anti-Christ) jews today (Revelation 2:9, 3:9; Isaiah 65:15). The anti-Christ jews are the image of the Beast of Revelation Chapter 13:14. . . . They cause the death of Christians.

—'Christian' Bible study Web site

Virtual haters twist scripture into a white-power pretzel. The most common version of their convoluted hermeneutics is "Identity" thought, a theology that uses the Bible to justify racism and to prophesy apocalyptic judgment against non-white, non-Aryan races.

Identity sites are often eye-glazingly similar. Scripture is quoted at great length and with great gusto. Jews are seen as the "anti-Christ" or "Satan's seed." Persons of color are deemed the "Unchosen" or "mud people." Self-preservation of the white race becomes an imperative for true "Christians," regardless of the personal costs involved.

Two different strands of Identity thought are currently in circulation—Christian Identity and Racial Identity.

The Christian Identity movement is linked to the doctrine of British Israelism that equates white people with the "true" Jews descended from the lost tribes of Israel. Racial Identity adherents believe that while today's Jews were once the true Jews of the Bible, Aryans have long since replaced them as God's chosen people. These variations engender competition and even hostility between the two groups.

Virtual Bigots, in All Sizes and Shapes

Like Identity adherents, Christian fundamentalist hate groups utilize the Bible to justify their beliefs. Unlike Identity members, however, fundamentalists focus much of their vitriol on gay and lesbian people and other sexual "abominations." While theological disagreement with sexual behavior does not, of course, qualify a church as a hate group, the ferocity of some online attacks have warranted sites like Westboro Baptist Church (WBC) a place on HateWatch's monitoring list.

Started by Fred Phelps, the infamous "God Hates Fags" demonstration leader, Westboro Baptist currently boasts two sites: www.godhatesfags.com and www.godhatesamerica. com. Phelps' grandson Ben, a Gen-Xer who works for a software company in Topeka, Kansas, maintains both. Phelps invites Web surfers to join fire-and-brimstone protests against gays and lesbians across the United States. "WBC to picket a million sodomite beasts at their pathetic Millennium March on Washington Apr. 30," reads one announcement. "WBC to picket Episcopal Fag Church General Convention in Denver, CO, Colorado Convention Center, July 5–14, in religious protest and warning," states another.

Virtual bigots like Phelps and World Church's LaRue come in all shapes, sizes, and religious leanings. But their intolerant attitudes do not in themselves qualify a site for monitoring, Brian Marcus points out. "We look for sites and groups that have online presences—not a catalog of every site with hate material on it." Serious hate sites are those that not only display overt hostility toward a person or group based on religion, gender, race, disability, or sexual orientation, but also use specific cyber-tactics that identify them as up-to-date and growing.

Strategies of Online Hate

The following strategies, culled from online research and from interviews with hate site Webmasters, anti-hate activists, and scholars, provide a sample of the tactics employed by virtual hate groups for recruitment, retention, and organizational growth.

Strategy One: Make Hate Noble

Virtual bigots like to couch hate in lofty terms. Emoting about freedom and racial self-preservation, they allude to a racial holy war and exhort others to join the struggle. Sacrifice becomes the mark of a dedicated racialist. Experiences of alienation, disapproval, or persecution are thus eased by the inner assurance that one is battling for a cause greater than oneself.

Some haters, Brian Marcus explains, see themselves as "Phineas Priests"—a biblical analogy from the tale of Phineas striking down those who consorted with the Midianites (Numbers 25:6–13) and being blessed by God for his courage. "This is read to justify racist actions taken by groups of haters," Marcus says, "and especially to sanctify those who take it upon themselves to commit these acts to bring about a 'proper' world."

Jerry's Aryan Battle Page gives violence a Phineasian twist with a monthly "Patriot of the White Race" award. In June 2000, Jerry honored a man named Mike Stehle for killing an "anti-racist" in supposed self-defense: "For his bravery in combat with our enemies, and for saving the lives of two other White racial patriots, Mike Stehle has become a hero of his people."

Strategy Two: Make Hate Anonymous

An anonymous bigot is more threatening than an identifiable one. The federal government recently confirmed this when it denied Klan members the right to wear hoods at public rallies. On the Internet, however, haters can reclaim the anonymity once granted by white robes. The Anti-Defamation League notes that items banned in public can now be symbolically donned in cyberspace—without legal or governmental reprisal.

Online Dangers for Teens

A growing venue for destructive influences is the Internet—and the drive is often aimed at teens.

"Hate groups typically target teens from 13 up to 24 years—they've had the most recruiting success in that age group," says David Goldman, executive director of HateWatch.org, an organization that monitors online hate groups.

"The kids who respond are typically confused, isolated, looking for something to belong to and these groups offer a solution, a way to feel good about themselves," explains Goldman. "They basically say, 'Hey, it's not you, it's them. They're the ones who are taking your jobs, or your future.' Some of them even have chat rooms that offer online classes in racist ideology."

There are roughly 600 hate groups based in the U.S., 450 of which have Web sites. All together the different groups oppose people from practically every race and ethnic background and religious organization that exists.

Maria Purdy, *Teen*, March 2000.

Virtual anonymity makes prosecution of haters difficult. In the United States, bigots cannot be taken to court unless their words are proven to be a "course of conduct" rather than a single occurrence. But with the emergence of technologies that offer substantial online anonymity, a bigot can repeatedly threaten someone without being readily identified.

Virtual anonymity also makes disclaimers easy. Hate leaders can disavow themselves from "random" shootings committed in their organizations' names because linking "lone wolf" haters to established Web sites is tricky, says Brian Marcus. Unless haters identify themselves or can be shown to have visited sites or conspired with others, determining which shooters are actually part of a group and which are mere isolated vigilantes becomes difficult.

Strategy Three: Make Hate Technological

In previous years, a hate group's success depended on the charisma of its leader. Today it depends on the technical savvy of its Webmaster. "Hate leaders don't have to have good looks or good public speaking ability anymore," says ADL's Jay Karman. "They need technical knowledge—and the ability to articulate a message through written words instead of speech."

In a field where technology changes almost daily, hate groups hunger for the skills to promote their message effectively. A few groups began using computers as early as 1983 to set up dial-in bulletin boards for promoting their ideas. Don Black, a former Grand Dragon of the KKK, was one of these early-bird haters, creating the first full-fledged Internet hate site in 1995. Today Black's Stormfront site continues to set the technological pace for white supremacists.

The Webmasters I interviewed displayed considerable technological creativity. Each claims to have learned Web design for the express purpose of putting up white supremacist sites. "I learned internet technology within the last month or so," writes LaRue. "I taught myself for the sole purpose of the [World Church of the Creator] Sisterhood Web site." Alex Curtis, Webmaster for the white supremacist site Nationalist Observer, says that while he learned computer basics for school, he developed Web site skills expressly for "White activism."

Putting up the site is just the beginning. High-powered sites often create their own "mirrors"—seemingly innocuous replications of a site designed to evade blocking. They also craft extensive link pages, multiple e-mail lists, and e-commerce arenas for selling white power paraphernalia. Don Black's Stormfront site even provides its own Internet service to avoid conflict with concerned Internet service providers.

Strategy Four: Make Hate Christian

"I am a Presbyterian and both racism and religion come naturally to me. . . . I put race first though, because biological extinction is right now the worst threat. Religion can always be relearned."

—Alex Curtis,
Webmaster for the Nationalist Observer

Is hate Christian? Identity and fundamentalist groups want you to think so. And many have the know-how to prove it. Westboro's Web master Ben Phelps could proof-text most seminary students into stunned silence. "Most people aren't supposed to believe the Bible," says Phelps, "because Jesus said that most people will go to hell. Matthew 7:13-14. . . . The goal is not to get everyone saved. The goal is to preach the truth to people and through that preaching God will call His elect into the fold."

Basing bigotry on the Bible helps virtual haters in two ways. First, it absolves them of responsibility for their hatred. Westboro's site claims to preach hate "because the Bible preaches hate. The maudlin . . . touchy-feely preachers of today's society are damning this nation and this world to hell."

Second, making hate "Christian" helps online groups recruit members from Bible-based and conservative churches. The line between respectful theological disagreement and out-and-out bigotry is sometimes a fine one. Haters such as Fred and Ben Phelps manipulate Christians into embracing hate in the name of biblical integrity.

Strategy Five: Make Hate Marketable

What's the best way to build a new business? Attract adolescents. Filmmakers do it. Evangelical mega-churches do it. Hate groups are doing it, too.

In an effort to make hate marketable, some sites sell computer games, such as White Power Doom, that have been altered to include African-Americans, Jews, and other minority groups as shooting targets. Other sites such as Resistance Records sell skinhead music that can be purchased with a standard credit card. The Resistance label is now owned by William Pierce, head of the incendiary Aryan Nations Web site and author of the racist treatise *The Turner Diaries*.

Still other sites provide links to the White Heritage Emporium, an e-shop that sells everything from Celtic jewelry to racist T-shirts. Don Black's Stormfront site even has a "white singles" dating section and a "kid's page" supposedly maintained by an 11-year-old boy named Derek. "I used to be in public school," says Derek. "It is a shame how many white minds are wasted in that system. I am now in home school. I no longer get beat up by gangs of non-whites and I spend of most my day learning, instead of tutoring the slowest kids in my class."

> *"Racism is a much smaller problem on the net than in the everyday world. Netizens are generally uninterested in all forms of physical difference."*

The Internet Does Not Foster Hate Speech

Charles Platt

In the following viewpoint, Charles Platt claims that hate speech on the Internet is not the problem that many anti-hate groups portray it as. In fact, he argues that most people who use the Internet are uninterested in physical differences such as ethnicity or nationality. Platt maintains that hate speech on the Internet will never be regulated, since it is protected by the First Amendment to the U.S. Constitution. Charles Platt is a contributing writer to *Wired* magazine.

As you read, consider the following questions:

1. Why might some racist newsgroups serve a useful purpose, according to Platt?
2. In Platt's opinion, how many of the 10,000 Usenet groups in existence have a racist agenda?
3. What kind of speech is not protected under the First Amendment, according to Scott Charney?

Excerpted from *Anarchy Online*, by Charles Platt. Copyright © 1996 by Charles Platt. Reprinted by permission of HarperCollins Publishers, Inc.

R abbi Marvin Hier is dean and founder of the Simon Wiesenthal Center and its Museum of Tolerance, located in the Los Angeles area. In May 1995 he testified before yet another Senate group discussing "dangerous" netspeech [speech on the Internet]. This time it was the Senate Subcommittee on Terrorism, Technology, and Government Information.

White Supremacists and Censorship

According to Hier, the Wiesenthal Center regularly monitors more than 240 hate groups, from neo-Nazi and Klan groups to Holocaust revisionists and Christian identity groups. Supposedly more than fifty of these groups were found

> utilizing various elements of cyberspace—from electronic bulletin boards to sophisticated Web sites on the Internet. . . . Cyberspace has suddenly empowered marginal local groups, be they overt white supremacists or militias with racist ties like the Northern Regional Militia of Michigan. These groups market nationally, inflammatory videos and computerized files which fuel a conspiratorial, rabidly anti-government and often violent world view.

It's true that white supremacist views are easy to find online, in newsgroups such as alt.politics.white-power. Rabbi Hier wasn't suggesting that these discussion groups should be banned, because he realized this would be unconstitutional. Instead, he urged that large Internet service providers should refuse to carry the groups, just as CNN or the *Washington Post* would refuse to carry advertising from "avowed racists or Nazis."

No one paid much attention to this suggestion, so the Wiesenthal Center escalated its attack. At the beginning of January 1996 it circulated a letter to hundreds of Internet service providers pressuring them to block access to any Usenet[1] groups or Web pages that were spawning grounds for hate speech. The center even offered to assist service providers "in drafting a code of ethics."

Bearing in mind that the Internet functions like a telephone system allowing people to exchange personal views,

---

1. Usenet is an online bulletin board system which features discussion forums on various topics of interest to users.

this call for a crack-down was like suggesting that AT&T should refuse to transmit phone calls from racists. Still, the Wiesenthal Center's press release attracted some sympathetic publicity, which faced Internet service providers with an unpleasant choice: impose a form of censorship, or be named as purveyors of anti-Semitic propaganda.

Most sites still refused to censor themselves. Some of them pointed out that the racist newsgroups actually serve a useful purpose, providing a forum where Holocaust revisionists can be debated and refuted. Even a group such as alt.politics.white-power usually contains dozens of messages arguing for tolerance and mocking the bigots.

Is Hate Speech Really Widespread?

There was a more fundamental issue, though, which no one mentioned: Is hate speech really as widespread as the Wiesenthal Center chose to imply?

At the Museum of Tolerance there is a map of America flagged with literally hundreds of "hate group" locations. By pressing numbered buttons, a visitor can call up more information about the groups. In many cases, this information reveals that "hate group" is not an accurate label. A group in New Jersey, for instance, turns out to consist of two alleged skinheads who burned down a warehouse more than five years ago and haven't been heard from since.

Online, maybe three or four out of more than 10,000 Usenet groups have a racist agenda. There are also some Web pages, the best-known being sponsored by Ernst Zundel, who has spent a large part of his life trying to debunk the Jewish Holocaust. In January 1996, shortly after the Wiesenthal Center circulated its press release, one of two telephone networks in Germany was persuaded by the German government to block access to Zundel's American Web site so that his writings could not be viewed by German citizens. Since German law prohibits certain forms of speech about Nazism, the action was legally justified. Within a day, however, American free-speech activists such as Declan McCullagh . . . started "mirroring" the Zundel site—duplicating its entire content on their own Web sites, even though they disapproved of what Zundel had to say. The message was clear: If one Web site was blacked out, half a dozen would take its place. A couple of weeks later, German authorities were forced to admit that their effort at censorship had been a failure.

Internet Postings Can Encourage Racial Dialogue: An Excerpt

I would just like to start by saying this: I am only 16 yrs old & maybe I shouldn't even be in this post room because it's for mothers—& I am not one. But, I just wanted to have my opinions be heard for once! I am a 16 yr old, white, female who definitely believes in interracial dating/marriages! Who are we to say if it is right or wrong just going by skin colors?! No one can honestly tell me that their favorite color is also the color of their skin. And, my point by saying that is then obviously it must be more than hatred because of skin color! I just wanted everyone out there who is racist to know that no matter what the color of your skin is you're still a person w/feelings, who can fall in love, raise children & be able to lead a happy life w/o having to hear ignorance from the people around you! Please E-MAIL me w/ your comments! Thanx

Jenis Bean, *New York Times*, March 8, 1998.

Here again, though, most press reports omitted to mention a pertinent fact: Most German citizens didn't bother to investigate Zundel's theories. One of the Web sites that made his text available logged fewer than 200 hits in a one-week period, even though the site had received national publicity. Most people simply weren't interested.

Virtual Threats Versus Real Threats

In fact, racism is a much smaller problem on the Net than in the everyday world. Netizens are generally uninterested in all forms of physical difference: age, disability, ethnicity, nationality, or race. It's common for people to swap messages without knowing any personal details about each other—even gender. Bearing this in mind, maybe it would make better sense for antiracism activists to forget about the Internet and concentrate on racism in the physical world, where it is a very legitimate cause for concern. Likewise, since bomb recipes and incitements to violence are extremely rare online, law enforcement would deploy its resources more effectively on the streets of any American city.

Of course, some senators refuse to see it that way. In the Senate subcommittee hearings on terrorism, technology, and government information, subcommittee chairman Arlen Specter suggested that some material on the Net—bomb-making information, in particular—poses a "clear and present danger" to American life. Since speech of this type would not be protected under the Constitution, Specter seemed to be finding a rationale here for censorship.

The Department of Justice respectfully disagreed. Robert Litt, a deputy assistant attorney general from the Criminal Division, told the senators what they should have already known: A bomb recipe, on its own, is protected speech. Moreover, when Litt was asked if he had any statistics or direct knowledge of any crime resulting from someone getting information from the Internet, he had to admit that there had never been a case of this kind. The "threat" of terrorist information on the Net was being exaggerated even more than the "threat" of hate speech or online pornography—and there was no way to pass a constitutional law against it, anyway.

In the words of Scott Charney, the leading expert on computer crime at the Department of Justice:

> Speech that incites imminent lawlessness or incitement to riot may not be protected, but generally speaking you cannot punish people even for reprehensible speech. As soon as you start talking about regulating speech, you have to ask who regulates it and where do you draw the lines, and you realize it's completely unworkable.

Probably Charney was speaking in legal terms when he made this statement, but controlling online content seems unworkable in practical terms, too. The German government couldn't figure out how to do it, Internet service provider CompuServe gave up after just a few weeks, and even if federal decency legislation survives legal challenges, there are some obvious ways to evade such restrictions.

The challenge of regulating the content of netspeech seems thorny at best and insoluble at worst. Could it be any easier to control access and distribution?

> "Never before in history has there been a
> better time to be a pedophile than today;
> both child pornography and child victims
> are readily available via computer."

Pedophiles on the Internet Are a Serious Problem

D. Douglas Rehman

D. Douglas Rehman is a founding member of the FBI's Operation Innocent Images Task Force, which specializes in the identification and investigation of individuals exploiting children via computers. In the following viewpoint, Rehman contends that the Internet has made it easy for pedophiles to exchange child pornography and entice children into online or real sexual encounters. He maintains that many of the children who become the victims of Internet pedophiles will later in life become child abusers themselves. Rehman argues that the United States needs federally funded task forces in order to catch and prosecute online child predators.

As you read, consider the following questions:

1. According to Rehman, how do Internet pedophiles persuade law-abiding citizens with attractions for children to exploit children online?
2. What is the typical profile of a computer pedophile, according to the author?
3. What type of child do sexual predators usually target, according to Rehman?

Excerpted from "Targeting Children on the Internet," D. Douglas Rehman's testimony before the U.S. House Committee on the Judiciary, Subcommittee on Crime, November 7, 1997.

Historically, pedophiles have sought children wherever they gather. School yards and playgrounds have been traditional hunting grounds, with the malls coming into vogue during the nineteen-nineties. At the end of the twentieth century, cyberspace is the child hangout. This provides the pedophile with virtually limitless possibility for victims and the ability to prowl anonymously from home with virtual safety from authorities.

Pedophiles Faced Many Challenges in the Past

One common trait of pedophiles is their collection of child pornography. They will amass large collections, but rarely, if ever, dispose of the child pornography. Until very recently, child pornography was extremely difficult to obtain with the primary source being European magazines and 8mm films that were published during the 1970's and 1980's. There was a limited number of these magazines in circulation and pedophiles, while wanting more child pornography, would not want to give up what they already had for new material. This made it virtually impossible for the trading of child pornography.

An even more basic problem for the pedophiles was a means to meet each other to trade child pornography, discuss seduction techniques, and for psychological validation of their behavior. Prior to the computer, this was very difficult and dangerous.

Computers Make It Easy

In the late nineteen-eighties and early nineties, computer technology advanced to the point where the European child pornography could be converted to readily reproducible computer image files. This, coupled with the widespread development of computer bulletin boards (BBS) [where users exchange messages], allowed for the commercial distribution of child pornography via computer. Pedophiles would have to pay fees, typically $50 or more per month, to be able to download this child pornography.

By 1994, the Internet service provider America Online (AOL) had created a very simple user interface that allowed persons with very limited computer skills to get online and navigate with ease. AOL also created "chat rooms" on their system. These electronic gathering places allow up to 23 members of AOL to gather and communicate electronically via keyboard. AOL also provided for the exchange of computer files between users via email attachments. In 1994, AOL only had approximately 500,000 members; in the late nineteen-nineties, AOL claims well in excess of nine million.

In 1994, child exploitation was becoming well established on AOL. Pedophiles roamed the various chat rooms in search of child victims and other pedophiles. In terms of its use by pedophiles, AOL became a victim of its own success. In 1994, I coined the term computer pedophiles to describe these online predators. The computer pedophiles from AOL that I have arrested and interviewed all claim that they did not get online for the child exploitation, but rather for the same reasons as legal users. They relate that once online, they came across the child exploitation and joined it. AOL has taken many steps to stop the exploitation of children, however, the computer pedophiles remain committed and find ways around these steps.

Child exploitation is not unique to AOL, the other online services have experienced problems from these online predators as well. In the last several years, the Internet has developed a well deserved reputation as a medium for child exploitation.

The Internet: Medium for Child Exploitation

The newsgroups are the electronic equivalent of cork boards; there are tens of thousands of newsgroups, covering virtually every topic imaginable. Internet users can post messages which other users can read. Additionally, computer image files can be posted and retrieved for viewing. Newsgroups carry important discussions of topics such as health matters, politics, and technology. Unfortunately, they also carry about a dozen newsgroups dedicated to the sexual exploitation of children. Within these groups, pedophiles regularly post nude images of children, frequently child pornography. They discuss seduction of children and look for victims.

Internet Relay Chat (IRC) provides "channels" that are similar to AOL's chat rooms. Unlike AOL, however, there is no regulation of the names of these channels or of the discussion topics. At any given time, there may be dozens of channels that graphically describe their content as being child exploitation; names such as "preteen sex pics" are commonplace. Through various software applications, computer pedophiles meeting in an IRC channel can exchange computer image files directly between their computers.

All of the above makes child pornography readily available online for anyone seeking it.

Online child exploitation is a double edged sword for law enforcement. For the first time in history, law enforcement has a powerful means for investigating child exploitation proactively. The same online anonymity that attracts the computer pedophiles also provides law enforcement officers with the ability to go undercover as child victims or as pedophiles. The reverse, however, is that computer pedophiles can readily obtain real victims and easily trade child pornography.

Pedophile Profiles

Perhaps the worst side effect of the online child exploitation is that it is self-perpetuating. I have arrested several computer pedophiles that would most likely never have engaged in child exploitation had they not gone online. Not all persons with pedophilia are child molesters or engaged in the collection of child pornography. Many are ordinary law abiding citizens who have a sexual attraction towards children, but control these desires and lead normal lives. When these individuals go online, they encounter computer pedophiles who extol the virtues of sex with children and provide them with child pornography. This psychological validation leads the person to believe that they aren't strange or different after all and that it is society, with its laws criminalizing sex with children and pornography involving children, that is wrong. They then begin the downward spiral into child exploitation, typically beginning by trading child pornography, progressing to sexually explicit online conversations with children, and eventually seeking child victims online for sex.

The most troubling aspect about the sexual victimization of boys is that some percentage will go on to molest children themselves. During post-arrest interviews, many pedophiles admit to having been sexually abused as children. While this abuse may help to explain their behavior, the sexual exploitation of children is a volitional act and is not excused by abuse suffered as a child. This factor, however, makes child exploitation unique among crimes: the victim may grow up to victimize.

The Orchid Club

In April 1996, a 10-year-old girl was invited to a slumber party at the home of another little girl in Greenfield, California. What her parents didn't know: The friend's father, Ronald Riva, was a member of the Orchid Club, an online group of men who met in pedophile chat rooms and used the Internet to swap pornography and true-life stories of child molestation.

That night, Riva and another club member, who was visiting, awoke the girl, then fondled her in front of a digital camera attached to a computer. The images of her molestation were broadcast to other members of the group, who watched the live event on their computers and responded interactively, typing in what they'd like to see happen next.

This shocking crime led to an investigation by U.S. Customs and other agencies, ending in the indictments of 16 members of the Orchid Club. The first known example of pedophiles using the Internet for real-life abuse of a child, the Orchid Club might be a barometer of where we are headed on the Internet.

Bob Trebilcock, *Redbook*, April 1, 1997.

Since becoming involved in the computer pedophile problem in 1994, I have spent a significant amount of my time conducting computer pedophile investigations. The vast majority of these investigations have been proactive; however, that has recently begun to change. When I first started working these investigations, many people in the criminal justice community believed that pedophiles were not acquiring victims online and that I was manufacturing crimes by my posing as a child. Unfortunately, since 1994 there has been an ever increasing number of reported victimizations of children that began online.

The typical computer pedophile is virtually always a white

male and usually middle or upper socio-economic status. The typical age range is approximately 25 to 45 years old, although computer pedophiles as young as nineteen and as old as mid-fifties have been prosecuted. As the generation that was exposed to computers as children ages, the upper age limit will disappear.

It is just as common for computer pedophiles to be married as not, although it is slightly less likely that they have children. Owing to their socio-economic status, white collar males are over represented. Very few computer pedophiles have a criminal history when they are arrested.

A Sexual Orientation

In understanding the behavior of pedophiles, it is important to first realize that it is a sexual orientation. Pedophiles are generally considered to be individuals that have a sexual attraction for children, under the age of 18, that are five or more years younger in age than the pedophile. This attraction is no different than the attraction that a heterosexual adult feels for opposite gender peers.

Pedophiles have very predictable behavior traits. These traits have been recognized by courts at all levels throughout the country through their upholding of search warrants that were based upon a pedophile profile. Of prime importance to law enforcement are studies conducted by various clinical researchers, that have found the average child molester will have more than seventy victims throughout their lifetime. Clinical studies and a wealth of experience by law enforcement officers throughout the country show that pedophiles will collect large amounts of child pornography that they rarely, if ever, dispose of.

Pedophiles are typically sexually obsessed with children. One computer pedophile that I arrested stated that he spends most of his day fantasizing about sex with children. Whenever he sees a child, whether in person, in a magazine, or on television, he begins to fantasize about having sex with that child. It is not uncommon for computer pedophiles to spend dozens of hours per week engaged in online child exploitation.

It is difficult to gain a clear picture of the child victims of the computer pedophiles, although they are generally between twelve and sixteen years of age and from middle socio-economic status homes. In many instances, the victims do not see themselves as such. An adolescent boy that is unsure of his sexual identity may explore homosexuality. These boys, afraid of harassment from their peers, look to the gay online community to discuss these issues. The computer pedophiles are all too aware of this and seek out these confused boys. They will provide them with dis-information and sexually victimize them. This victimization is rarely reported; either the boys believe they are gay and therefore they see the sex as consensual, or the boys are embarrassed by what happened and are afraid of peer harassment.

The victimizations of girls, as with boys, is most often reported by a parent or other concerned adult. The girls typically do not see themselves as victims. They view the pedophile as a prince that will take them away to live a grand life in a castle.

Pedophiles in general, and computer pedophiles in particular, are very good at identifying potential victims. Typically, they look for children that are loners. On a playground, they would look for the child that is apart from the others, the child that is the last to be picked for a team. These same vulnerable children can be found online in great numbers. The children may spend large amounts of time online, often looking for acceptance and understanding. The computer pedophiles seek out these children and fulfill the children's emotional needs. By fulfilling these needs, the computer pedophile gains the child's trust which allows the pedophile to talk the victim into engaging in sexual acts. After being sexually violated, many victims cannot articulate why they engaged in the sexual acts with the pedophile. In retrospect, they realize it was a mistake.

Sex and Children

From the time that pornographic magazines were first published, adolescent males have sought out these kinds of materials. Pedophiles have always been aware of this and now have a readily available supply of potential victims online. In the course of my undercover activities as a child, I have received thousands of pornographic computer image files, both adult and child. Often the pedophiles will furnish adult pornography to a potential victim as a means of opening communications about sex. Very often, computer pedophiles will supply potential victims with large amounts of child pornography. By showing the child large numbers of other similar children engaging in sexual acts, the pedophile seeks to show the victim that such behavior is normal and pleasurable. . . .

Computer pedophiles prowl the online services and the Internet seeking victims. They will answer postings by children seeking pen pals. They will go into "teen" chat rooms. In an effort to gain the child's confidence, they will sometimes portray children themselves, later introducing their "father", "uncle", or "friend."

Unfortunately, sex pervades our society. Our children are bombarded with sex on television, the movies, in music, in advertising, and virtually every other facet of their lives. Studies show that children are becoming sexually active at younger ages. While the child's reasoning abilities and decision-making processes are not yet fully formed, the child is at least sexually curious. This is a pedophile's delight. Many pedophiles, particularly the boylovers, find their child victims in adult sex chat rooms.

When posing as a potential child victim online, it is routine to be simultaneously contacted by ten or more pedophiles seeking cybersex, or sometimes real sex, with a child. It is very much akin to a shark feeding frenzy. . . .

A Law Enforcement Solution

The child exploitation problem is well beyond the resources of state and local law enforcement. A major influx of federal dollars is needed to combat these henious crimes. In cyberspace, pedophiles routinely cross jurisdictional lines. In the real world, owing to our highly mobile society, pedophiles regularly cross jurisdictional lines. Federally funded task forces must be established throughout the country. The funding must completely underwrite the costs, including officers' salaries. Likewise, additional federally funded and highly trained prosecutors are needed at both the federal and state level to prosecute the avalanche of child exploitation cases.

Unlike drug trafficking, there is no one looking to take the place of an arrested pedophile. A concentrated effort at all levels, aimed at pedophiles engaged in child exploitation, could have significant impact on the problem.

Never before in history has there been a better time to be a pedophile than today; both child pornography and child victims are readily available via computer. Never before in history has law enforcement had an opportunity to impact child exploitation as can be done now via computer. For many years, we have been waging a war against illegal drugs. The time has come for a declaration of war against child exploitation.

*"There is little evidence that we are
genuinely menaced [by Internet pedophiles].
Statistics are scarce. . . . Arrests have been
made—but for abduction? Assault? Rape?
Sexual molestation? Well, no."*

The Extent of Internet
Pedophilia Is Exaggerated

James R. Kincaid

*James R. Kincaid teaches at the University of Southern Cal-
ifornia and is the author of several books including* Erotic In-
nocence: The Culture of Child Molesting. *Kincaid argues in the
following viewpoint that most children are abducted and
sexually abused by family members, not by strangers lurking
on the Internet. He claims that despite the lack of evidence
that pedophiles on the Internet pose a serious threat, many
law enforcement groups and child advocacy organizations
are actively pursuing arrests of men they believe pose a danger to children. Kincaid asserts that focusing attention on
Internet predators takes resources away from solving real
problems such as child abuse within the family.*

As you read, consider the following questions:
1. According to Kincaid, what is "Innocent Images"?
2. What is "panic talk," according to the author?
3. According to the Chicago Advocacy Center, what
   percentage of its last four thousand child sex abuse
   cases involved the Internet in some way?

Reprinted, with permission, from James R. Kincaid, "Hunting Pedophiles on the
Net." This article first appeared in *Salon.com* at http://www.Salon.com. An online
version remains in the *Salon* archives.

For many of us (geeks excepted), the Internet is big and mysterious and, for the most part, unknowable. It can be a very scary place. We don't have much difficulty imagining wicked pedophiles infiltrating chat rooms where young girls and boys hang out. We can see these cyberpredators patiently gaining the innocent trust of their victims and then luring them into sexually exploitative or even fatal meetings. It is easy to conjure up the precise details of Internet dangers to our children, especially with the help of organizations created to warn us about such things. We have learned to fear Internet pirates, poised to steal our money or our privacy; it's natural enough that we should believe in electronic kidnappers and do whatever is necessary to protect our children from them.

Innocent Images

And we have, on the local and, most emphatically, on a national level. In 1994, after the alleged abduction by way of the Internet of 10-year-old Bruce Burdinski in Maryland, the FBI announced that it would become proactive in regulating Internet traffic in images and bodies. A year later, the agency launched "Innocent Images," a program designed to train law enforcement officials to imitate young girls and boys in chat rooms in an attempt to catch electronic stalkers. The idea was to lure the would-be molesters out of hiding and into meetings—and then arrest them.

According to the FBI's Peter Gullotta, the program has been a great success, resulting in 515 arrests and 439 convictions since 1995. (Former Infoseek executive Patrick Naughton, sentenced to five years' probation in August 2000, was arrested in an Innocent Images sting operation.) In 10 division offices across the country (the headquarters is in Baltimore), the FBI now trains specially deputized workers with the support of a special congressional grant of $10 million. Innocent Images initiated 700 investigations in fiscal 1998 and 1,500 the next year.

Gullotta carefully notes that the increase in cases, some of which may be based on nothing more than an anonymous tip, doesn't indicate a huge increase in the number of pedophiles but simply reflects a greater number of "efforts to catch them." He does, however, express unambiguous confidence that the people being caught are indeed predators and that the Innocent Images program is effectively addressing a genuine menace.

A Lack of Evidence

The problem is that there is little evidence that we are genuinely menaced. Statistics are scarce, anecdotes easy to come by. Arrests have been made—but for abduction? Assault? Rape? Sexual molestation? Well, no. The Burdinski case that inspired the Innocent Images program was never brought to court or solved, so we simply do not know what happened: The boy was never found. He may indeed have been abducted by way of a chat room, but we don't know that.

Gullotta says the FBI has no figures on how many children are abducted or met by way of chat rooms. The National Center for Missing and Exploited Children doesn't have any figures either, though it does have a CyberTipline, where concerned citizens can call in suspicious things they spot on the Internet: child pornography, prostitution, child-sex tourism, molestation and enticement.

The CyberTipline has recorded 1,848 tips concerning enticement in the past two years, but that's only 12 percent of the total tips taken by the service, and no one knows how many of those complaints are duplicates, mistakes or malicious calls meant to do harm to enemies.

It would seem that at this point, invested as we are in this crisis, we are simply trusting our instincts—our worst fears—which is something we have done before, particularly in the area of child sexual safety. In the past decade or so, we have gone on a lot of crusades in the name of protecting our children from sexual predators: We have raided preschools, the dens of witches and our own memories. We have managed to make a number of arrests too, very often of innocent people, and have disrupted lives, scared kids and separated them from parents.

But we haven't seemed to learn that our ability to convince ourselves that a threat exists is no guarantee that there is one; our ability to make arrests does not mean crimes have been committed; our determination to protect our children does not mean we are doing so. Satanic ritual abuse, we recall, did not exist at all—nowhere, not once, not to anybody: So says the FBI.

The Burden of Proof

This is not to say that Internet predators do not exist or that the Innocent Images program is not a good idea. But a few compelling questions might not be misplaced in an atmosphere of panic, questions like: What evidence is there that children have been lured into meetings by Internet predators? How large is this problem, if indeed it is a problem? Are we wise to devote our resources to this problem rather than to others? Can we be sure we are not creating the crime, luring people out of hiding and arresting them for their fantasies? Is there something amiss in the idea of a crime against a child that involves no child, only trained imposters? (Naughton argued, through his lawyer, that he, like so many others, was involved in role-playing on the Net, fully aware that his cyberpals might not be who they said they were.)

The Real Monsters Are Sitting on the Living-Room Couch

The biggest threat to children's well-being is the adults who are supposed to protect them. The image of a dark, ravening stranger, loitering in sunglasses and a trenchcoat in school yards, playgrounds and chat rooms is much less threatening to our image of the nuclear family than the stark reality of a father forcing his 10-year-old daughter to perform oral sex on him. The right wing, with its family-values rhetoric, can't use its favorite technique of scapegoating gays and liberals to explain that away.

Wyn Hilty, www.taasa.org/library/internet_abuse/internet_blame_game.htm, 2000.

We cannot prove that crimes are being committed, but surely the burden of proof should be on those inaugurating programs to wipe out the menace. It should not be enough that the menace is horrifying or even horrifyingly convincing: That may simply mean that the image fits current cultural mythology, a mythology that, in this area, may be driven partly by panic.

The FBI points to the number of people arrested as unambiguous evidence both of the success of the Innocent Images program and of the magnitude of the problem: We wouldn't be catching them if they weren't there. This seems altogether logical, but it may also be altogether circular. Certainly Innocent Images agents have nabbed people who have crossed state lines to meet their chatmates and, presumably, engage in illegal sexual activities with them. There is, for most people, strong presumptive support for the program right there.

Maybe so, but we still ought to ask certain skeptical questions, just so they get asked. Remember the McMartin Preschool.[1] We owe it to ourselves and to our children to be certain we are not assuming at the start that there is a problem without any evidence that one exists, apart, perhaps, from our need to imagine one.

Panic Talk

We ought to note that the discourse surrounding this problem follows the predictable path of panic talk. First of all, we are told that this problem is not just any problem, but that it is menacing, sneaky, "widespread and growing." "Many parents," says the National Center for Missing and Exploited Children, "have a false sense of security regarding the risks to their children in cyberspace." And FBI Director Louis Freeh concurs, telling Congress that "no greater danger" for children exists in computerland.

Cyberspace is portrayed as a dark sea filled with piranhas: Agent Gullotta gleefully says, "It's like fishing in a pond full of hungry fish. Every time you put a line with live bait in there, you're going to get one." This kind of talk can become reckless and can cause such alarm in good and caring people that they act to protect their children and ask questions later—or not at all.

1. On August 12, 1983, Ray Johnson—a school aid at the McMartin Preschool in Los Angeles County, California—was accused of abusing children at the school. The case became famous because it brought to light the way children are interrogated in sexual abuse cases. Although extensive media coverage implied wrongdoing, Johnson was never convicted.

Creating Crime Where None Exists

We ought to ask, for instance, whether those who are arrested for the crime of crossing a state line to pursue sex with a minor would have done so without this inducement. Gullotta gives the following typical profile for those arrested: A white male, age 25–45, intelligence and income above average, with no previous record in this area (or, often, any other).

When asked about the "no previous record" issue, Gullotta says that those caught have either been very "lucky" previously or, if this is their first venture, very "unlucky." The FBI claims that it is digging out those dangerous, innocent-looking "people next door" who are all the more lethal because they do not seem to be the type to do such a thing and have never done it before.

Maybe, but it is also possible that the FBI is helping create the crimes it is then "solving." Psychologist David Greenfield argues (in a ZDNet News essay by Lisa M. Bowman) that "these people may have been cajoled into acting out in ways they normally wouldn't." We cannot know that, and it will seem to many of us that the high conviction rate for crossing state lines to meet underage chat room companions (as high as 99 percent, Gullotta says) renders such questions moot.

Perhaps, but we should at least wonder about a conviction rate based almost entirely on plea bargains and on the assumption that the people going to these meetings weren't lured there. Very few cases go to trial, which, for the FBI, is evidence of guilt. "The Internet brings these guys out; it's that simple," says FBI agent Randy Aden. They are guilty, know it and flinch from having their filthy talk read out to juries, he assumes.

Plea Bargains Distort the Problem

Another possibility is that those nabbed, wanting to minimize exposure and thus avoid a trial, are very eager candidates for plea bargains. They admit to the lesser charge (going to the meeting) in return for having weightier charges (possession, endangerment) dropped. Such was the case with Naughton, who faced up to 35 years in prison if convicted. The deal he accepted—a guilty plea to possession of child pornography, which resulted in a sentence of five years of probation and a $20,000 fine—gave him an end to the battle.

Without knowing how great a threat is posed by Internet sex predators, it is downright bizarre that we concentrate so much time and money on hunting them down. Especially when we are aware, painfully so, of much greater threats to our children and fail to give them the same kind of attention.

In the whole range of abuse problems that come to the attention of social service agencies, sexual child abuse is the most rare. It ranks far below neglect, emotional abuse and physical abuse, finishing in a dead heat with "other." Yet sexual child abuse attracts almost all our attention and most of the money spent on child abuse. Why? We should not assume that the reasons are obvious or good ones. It would be irresponsible and cruel not to press further.

Family More of a Threat than Internet Pedophiles

We do know that FBI statistics on "classic abductions" of children (i.e., those that involve strangers taking a child physically away and doing harm) total between 100 and 200 per year—it is not known how many involve the Internet. Put those figures in perspective: There are 350,000 intrafamily abductions per year. Somewhere between 40,000 and 80,000 of the kids abducted by family are physically abused, between 3,000 and 20,000 sexually molested. (Because these figures are compiled with numbers from different agencies with different reporting schemes and, more important, different definitions of the key terms, it is perhaps more accurate to use mean figures here: About 60,000 of the kids abducted by family members are physically abused; roughly 12,000 are sexually molested.)

The Chicago Child Advocacy Center reports that of the last 4,000 child sex abuse cases it has handled, 0.13 percent have involved the Internet in some way. We might wonder what problem we are pursuing and whether all this attention to monstrous electronic strangers isn't, in part, a way to avoid looking inside our own homes and minds.

If we have evidence that sexual abuse is not the greatest

problem facing our children, and that sexual abusers are almost always (up to 99 percent of the time) within the family or the family circle, why do we land so heavily—almost exclusively—on the image of the abductor? Surely we should ask whether this Internet predator isn't simply the latest version of the figure we keep seeking out, the Other, the monster who is threatening our kids. We should at least wonder if it's the kids we are protecting by this maneuver.

No one would argue that we should ignore threats to our children or that any child's right to happiness (and safety) is trivial. This is not an issue of mathematics but of the motivations and good sense of the adult population. We don't do ourselves or our children any favors by focusing relentlessly on problems that serve mostly to keep us from worrying about what's inside our favored institutions, institutions like the family. By casting the problem in Gothic terms—"Kill the beast"—we do not encourage careful or even compassionate thinking.

Children have real problems in our culture, problems less spectacular but just as crippling as any Internet abduction. We need always to have them in mind, the children who are beaten, ignored, neglected and shut out, denied decent education, hope and love. We must answer to them as well, and right now our loud protestations of virtue, our declarations of willingness to protect, must ring hollow.

Who is being served by our willingness to rush headlong after problems, even before we know the problems exist? All it takes to get our undivided attention, it seems, is a problem that is spectacular, sexualized and far from home.

We need to ask hard questions of our policing agencies and be skeptical even of our own most heated fears. We've been down that road before, and we ought to see that nobody is served by such trips. This is what William Dworin, retired Los Angeles police detective, says: "We won't be able to prove that a child was saved from molestation because of these proactive investigations, but the price is worth the effort."

That is precisely the sort of thinking we ought to take to the court of reason. Let's have some proof that the problem exists. Let's be sure the price is worth the effort, whatever that means.

Periodical Bibliography

The following articles have been selected to supplement the diverse views presented in this chapter. Addresses are provided for periodicals not indexed in the *Readers' Guide to Periodical Literature*, the *Alternative Press Index*, the *Social Sciences Index*, or the *Index to Legal Periodicals and Books*.

A. Armstrong and J. Hagel	"The Real Value of Online Communities," *Harvard Business Review*, May/June 1996.
Mimi Avins	"Dates That Click," *Los Angeles Times*, February 13, 2000. Available from Times Mirror Square, Los Angeles, CA 90053.
Jane E. Brody	"Cybersex Gives Birth to a Psychological Disorder," *New York Times*, May 16, 2000.
Maura Kelly	"An Interview with Parry Aftab: Making the Web Safe for Children," www.Salon.com, 2000.
Steven Levy	"Breathing Is Also Addictive," *Newsweek*, December 30, 1996–January 6, 1997.
Michel Marriott	"Frank Racial Dialogue Thrives on the Web," *New York Times*, March 8, 1998.
Neal Pierce	"Beyond the Digital Divide," *Liberal Opinion*, March 6, 2000. Available from 108 E. Fifth St., Vinton, IA 52349.
David Streitfeld	"A World Wide Web of Workalcoholics," *Washington Post*, February 21, 2000. Available from 1150 15th St. NW, Washington, DC 20071.
Adam D. Thierer	"Don't Create a New Entitlement to Close a Gap That the Marketplace Already Is Filling," *Insight*, September 4, 2000. Available from 3600 New York Ave. NE, Washington, DC 20002.
Bob Trebilcock	"Child Molesters on the Internet: Are They in Your Home?" *Redbook*, April 1, 1997.
Langdon Winner	"Electronically Implanted 'Values,'" *Technology Review*, February/March 1997.

CHAPTER 2

How Will the Internet Affect American Institutions?

Chapter Preface

Nearly half of the voters participating in Arizona's 2000 Democratic presidential primary cast their votes via the Internet. Arizona is the first state to use "e-voting" in an attempt to make it easier to vote, thereby encouraging more American citizens to participate in elections.

E-voting is just one of the ways that the Internet has been used in an effort to improve American democracy. Another way that democracy is being influenced by the Internet is through the proliferation of websites designed to provide a forum for political discussion. Unlike mainstream television or newspapers, the Internet is not controlled by a central editorial board, which allows more diverse opinions to flourish. Such open communication, Internet advocates maintain, is vital to democracy. In addition, the Internet allows concerned citizens to contact their government representatives via e-mail. Tracy Westen, president of the Center for Governmental Studies, an organization that researches ways to improve government, argues that the Internet can revitalize American democracy by encouraging "two-way communications: from candidate to candidate, from voter to candidate, and from voter to voter."

Not everyone thinks that the Internet can be used to improve democracy, however. Many analysts argue that the Internet does not provide a forum for diverse citizens to express their political views. Only those with financial means to buy computers have easy access to the Internet, they claim. Georgie Anne Geyer, a syndicated columnist, contends that "the Internet divides people, most importantly by class." In consequence, many critics argue that political activism conducted over the Internet will be guided by the more affluent and will pursue goals that are important only to that segment of the populace.

For good or ill, the Internet is destined to play a significant role in American public life, from changing the way that citizens vote to reshaping relationships between representatives and their constituents. The authors in the following chapter discuss the Internet's effect on American institutions.

> *"Providing schools with ubiquitous high-speed access to the Internet is clearly a means to promote inquiry and learning in the classroom and beyond the limitations of textbooks."*

The Internet Can Improve Education

Bruce O. Barker

Bruce O. Barker contends in the following viewpoint that the Internet can improve education by creating active learners who are responsible for their own learning. The Internet provides an electronic space where anyone, anywhere can access information, establish virtual learning communities with others, and work on collaborative projects, he maintains. Schools that provide Internet access, Barker asserts, also teach students important skills that they will need in a technology-based society. Bruce O. Barker is dean of the College of Education at Southern Utah University.

As you read, consider the following questions:
1. What is "distance learning," according to Barker?
2. What was the ratio of Internet-connected computers to students in 1999, according to the author?
3. According to Barker, what are "technonauts"?

Reprinted, with permission, from "Anytime, Anyplace Learning," by Bruce O. Barker, *Forum of Applied Research and Public Policy*, Spring 2000. Endnotes in the original version have been omitted from this reprint.

Few educational innovations in recent years have caught the interest of educational policymakers like distance learning. State-sponsored curriculum reforms, reductions in state fiscal revenues, teacher shortages, and an increased desire to broaden educational opportunities for all students have increased the opportunities for using distance learning to deliver instruction.

Distance Learning Defined

Distance learning is typically defined as the delivery of live instruction from one site to another, or to multiple sites, using audio or video technologies that allow the teacher and students at different sites to interact with each other. Recent developments in communications technology are expanding this basic definition. In the past, if distance learning was to be interactive, students and their teachers separated by distance had to meet at the same time via telecommunications. Under ideal conditions, students at any one site were provided direct contact with their instructor, as well as communication with students at other remote sites during the instructional process.

Increasingly, however, programs today do not require that participants meet at the same time. Such programs allow virtually "anytime, anyplace learning." This is particularly true of courses delivered over the Internet.

Today's digital revolution and the exponential growth of the Internet have given rise to a vast number of websites and electronic databases that combine text, audio, graphics, and video information, which can be downloaded and viewed on a personal computer. This allows individuals to gather information, keep current on virtually any topic of interest, and communicate with others across the country or around the world on their own time and at their own pace.

Not surprisingly, time-insensitive distance learning via the Internet is growing much more rapidly as an educational delivery medium than such time-sensitive delivery systems as satellite, fiber optic, cable, or other TV-based networks. In addition, the infrastructure and telecommunications costs of the Internet are less than other distance learning systems.

With the ever-increasing number of Web-based courses,

as well as the exponential growth of the Web as an information resource, Bill Rodrigues, vice president and general manager for Dell Computer's K–12 education business unit, offers a more expanded definition of distance learning:

> The best term to describe distance learning is anytime, anywhere learning because that implies that learning is not confined to the four walls of the classroom. Through distance learning, learning can take place from anywhere on campus, from home, through peers around the world, through the Internet, or even from a hospital room. Distance learning means not necessarily having a teacher and students physically in the classroom but learning from anywhere via the use of a computer.

Learning anytime, anywhere is happening today, and will happen more in the future as access to information and communication improves. There are already a number of online high schools. More important, however, more and more schools across the country are connecting to the Internet, allowing students to learn on their own as well as join other learners in virtual communities linked by technology.

Online High

Choice 2000, a public charter school in Riverside, California, presents itself as the first totally online public high school in the United States. The school offers a fully certified 7th-through-12th-grade curriculum, plus adult education programs, online via the Web. The programs are accredited by the Western Association of Schools and Colleges. Tuition, textbooks, and software are free to residents of California, while the basic tuition for out-of-state residents is $175 per class for a nine-week semester, with additional costs for mailing textbooks and materials, depending on location.

Online attendance requirements are similar to traditional school requirements; students are expected to log-on every school day, Monday through Friday. Classes are held in a live email conference chat-room format with as many as 40 students and a teacher connected at one time. In this format, teachers can present information, hold electronic discussions, or answer student questions online; additionally, teachers and students can communicate regularly via email.

Students complete assignments from the teacher, as well as assignments delivered through a computer-based education and communications network that provides self-paced, interactive courses. Although the students do not travel to school to take classes, the school nonetheless offers extracurricular school activities such as dances, field trips, and picnics to encourage the students to interact socially.

Across the United States, a small but growing number of other online schools have been recently established in addition to Choice 2000. Gifted students often prefer online schools because such schools allow students to progress faster academically than traditional schools might permit. Students with physical or mental disabilities sometimes turn to distance learning to avoid the stigma they fear they might encounter at a more traditional school. Other students prefer distance learning because they are attracted by the computer technology. Students in remote areas often choose distance learning to avoid long bus rides. And increasingly, students and parents alike are turning to distance learning to assuage their fears of violence on campus.

The Three Ws

While a number of online high schools have been established, the fact remains that they affect few students. Although additional online schools will surely be established, the likelihood of broad appeal to either students or parents is unlikely.

Of greater interest is the use of the World Wide Web as a distance learning tool to benefit teachers and students in traditional school settings across the entire K–12 curriculum. Providing schools with ubiquitous high-speed access to the Internet is clearly a means to promote inquiry and learning in the classroom and beyond the limitations of textbooks. The promise of rapid access to the World Wide Web empowers teachers and students to access enormous amounts of information and interactive resources.

Internet access enables all students in all classrooms in all schools to become active distance learners. Likewise, teachers can more readily expand learning opportunities for their students. Through access to the vast amount of resources on the

Internet, teachers in Web-supported classrooms are able to:
- Take students on electronic field trips,
- Clarify and expand new information learned in the classroom,
- Design lesson plans and enrichment materials in support of local and national learning standards,
- Arrange for students to participate in collaborative projects with students around the world, and
- Expose students to the massive collections of information regularly being added to the Internet.

Web Connections

One of the top goals of the U.S. Department of Education was to connect every classroom to the Internet by 2000. Although that goal was not achieved, the number of Internet-connected classrooms has increased sharply in recent years, and essentially all classrooms are expected to have Internet access early in the 21st century.

Worldwide, nearly 200 million people have access to the Internet—with 80 million users in the United States alone. In a recent study published in *Education Week*, researchers found that 51 percent of American classrooms reported having Internet connections in 1998, an increase of 27 percent from the previous year. The same study indicated that 49 percent of the nation's schools have high-speed connection to the Web. Furthermore, the ratio of Internet-connected computers to students was 1 to 13.6 nationwide in 1999, a marked improvement from 1998 when the average ratio was 1 to 19.7. Ratios vary considerably among the states, with Delaware reporting the best ratio of 1 Web-connected computer to 5.6 students, North Carolina reporting 1 to 25.4, and the District of Columbia reporting the worst ratio of 1 to 31.1.

Virtual Learning Communities

The Web is the medium by which Internet resources can be organized for information access and exchange. It is attractive to students and teachers because someone else has already done the work of locating and organizing meaningful collections of Internet resources. Using the Web, teachers and students can more easily form learning communities extending far beyond the classroom. They can free themselves of the bonds of geographical isolation, which can be critical in rural schools.

The Internet Helps Teachers

The Net makes it cheaper and easier for teachers to learn from others, to form networks outside their own schools, to trade ideas, and to learn from the best practitioners in their field. Teachers can use it to communicate with other teachers, share best practices, arrange joint field trips, follow up on contacts they made at teachers' conferences—and of course to find all kinds of information and instructional material. They can also reach out to invite experts or business leaders to come in and speak to a class—or at least send information. (Smart companies will be eager to communicate with the customers and potential employees of the future!)

Esther Dyson, *Release 2.0: A Design for Living in the Digital Age*, 1997.

These virtual communities emerge in cyberspace whenever a group of learners in different locations carries on public discussions with sufficient human interaction to form learning relationships. Teachers and students in virtual learning communities use words and images on screen to exchange greetings, engage in intellectual discourse, conduct meetings, share knowledge, offer emotional support, make plans, brainstorm ideas, learn about other cultures, and otherwise broaden their mental horizons. In fact, they do much of what teachers and students might do in traditional classrooms, but they do it online and thereby extend the community of the classroom into the community of the world.

Internet Strategies

As a teaching and learning tool, the Internet permits interactive, nonlinear navigation through its pages, and it activates the senses of sight, sound, and cognitive reasoning, engaging students and creating active learners. The Internet allows for a variety of learning strategies. Judi Harris at the University of Texas identifies seven educational activity structures that can be incorporated into Internet teaching strategies:

- Information searches—students are given clues and must use resources, either on or off the Internet, to solve the problem.
- Electronic process writing—students post their written work, such as poems or essays, to a user group for critical feedback.
- Sequential creations—students begin or add to the work of others. An example might be a poem about world peace that "virtually" travels to many locations, with new lines being added at each stop along the way.
- Parallel problem solving—students in several locations work separately on solving the same problem and then electronically share their findings, methods, and analyses.
- Virtual gatherings—students from different geographic locations gather electronically to discuss a problem or question.
- Simulations—students access or create virtual worlds that allow them to explore such things as climate-change modeling and plant-growth modeling, or simulate space shuttle launches, historical space missions, space colony design, ozone-layer repair, and stock market investments.
- Social action projects—students engage in such activities as fund raising, ecology projects, and issues awareness.

In Loco Parentis

The Internet is a decentralized conglomeration of networks with no central administrative headquarters or governing body. By design, no one fully monitors or censors information entered to servers interconnected around the world. As a result, students not only can access unlimited information on almost every wholesome topic known to humanity, they can access information on almost every deviant and perverse topic as well. To guard against this, schools can use filters to screen or prevent access to controversial topics. Most schools have adopted appropriate-use policies, which typically stipulate that students shall not intentionally access or download any text file or picture, or engage in any conference, that includes pornography, violence, racism, anarchy, treason, or discrimination.

The Internet is today and tomorrow's tool for communicating with others, irrespective of distance and time. While some skeptics may criticize the computer as a form of depersonalized learning, Internet-connected computers actually do more to put learners in contact with other learners than any other telecommunications medium available. The Internet promotes the concept of a community of learners, not only in the traditional classroom, but in virtual learning communities linked together by state, national, and global connections.

Once students have full access to the Internet, changes are certain to occur in the teaching and learning process. Under the guidance of skilled teachers, students will become "technonauts." Much like astronauts who explore unknown worlds, technonauts are knowledge explorers who use technology to find, exchange, and analyze information. As technonauts, students will take more responsibility for their own education and will collaborate with others to find information outside the classroom. The more traditional roles of teachers and students will break down—in some cases, students will become teachers while teachers become students. In the classroom, teachers will serve as facilitators, guides, and co-learners.

The Web is the most pervasive and perhaps easiest tool for promoting distance learning in the world today. It can take students beyond the boundaries of the classroom or the confines of the standard school day. Regularly updated websites are much more current and timely than printed textbooks. The opportunity for students and teachers, at the click of a mouse, to explore topics of interest from databases around the world empowers them to grasp a vision of learning beyond anything that was considered possible even a few years ago.

As education moves into the 21st century, students need to develop skills and expertise in accessing, exchanging, and analyzing digital information if they hope to be successful in the world and workplace of the future. Without doubt, they need exposure to today's telecommunications tools to master the knowledge and technology that will shape tomorrow's society.

Just as the technology of the printing press revolutionized learning in the 15th century, so the technology of the Internet too, will revolutionize learning in the 21st century. As the Internet evolves and students and teachers become increasingly proficient at navigating its databases and services, the information of the world will truly be at their fingertips—anytime, anyplace.

> *"With no solid proof computers boost students' learning, the high cost of maintaining and upgrading a gaggle of laptops, scanners, and CD-ROMs may not be worth the payoff."*

The Internet Has Not Improved Education

David Kushner

In the following viewpoint, David Kushner contends that the Internet and other digital technologies actually interfere with learning because they encourage students to absorb information without understanding it or questioning its accuracy. He argues that most high school students use the Internet not for educational purposes but to exchange gossip and tease one another. Most important, Kushner maintains that technology can undermine education by convincing students that learning how computers work is more important than understanding how to use them to learn. David Kushner is an editor and writer for *Spin* magazine.

As you read, consider the following questions:
1. What technologies have been called upon in the past to reinvent education, according to Kushner?
2. According to the author, what happens when a technological glitch occurs in a wired classroom?
3. What is the author concerned about when one of Celebration's students downloads information from a James Joyce website?

Reprinted, with permission, from "The Dog Ate My Hard Drive," by David Kushner, *Spin*, April 1998.

The dream for the school of tomorrow opens on an old, familiar man from yesterday. Standing near an architect's sketch of a space-age city, Walt Disney, the late animator who gave us the world's most famous mouse, talks of building "a community that more people will talk about than anywhere else." At its heart will be an educational wonderland. As he fades, we cut to today, where happy residents in brightly lit living rooms extol the virtues of safe streets, good teachers, and high-speed cable modems.

Virtual Reality Shakespeare

This sales pitch loops a couple dozen times a day in the preview center at Celebration, the town Walt Disney Imagineering recently built near the Magic Kingdom in Orlando, Florida. Every day, herds of sun-pinked tourists wander in for a quick tour. What they get is the same hype that's buzzing across the country: High-tech schools, like the one here, will not only better equip students for the computer age, they'll make them smarter. Now, 30 years after Disney first imagined EPCOT (the Experimental Prototype Community of Tomorrow), a new team of dreamers is developing the model smart-school in Celebration's immaculate 'burb.

Since its ribbon was cut in 1996, Celebration has received plenty of attention for the sheer kitsch value of 1,200 people living in a theme-park town. A more dynamic story, however, has been unfolding in Celebration's K–12 public school. While Celebration's homes hearken back to Norman Rockwell Americana—a product of New Urbanism's interest in renewing "community"—its school is pure Jetsonian Utopia. Armed with a stockpile of techno gadgetry, students will soon perform virtual-reality Shakespeare, collaborate with students in Malaysia, and analyze pond scum with electronic probes.

"Most schools still teach like it's the 1940s," says Larry Rosen, the evangelical education professor who helped plan Celebration's Teaching Academy. "Would you rather have doctors operating on you with modern equipment or with technology from the '40s?" As other schools scramble to boot up, Disney, with the backing of the local Osceola County and the Celebration Company, has pooled $30 million to create the most wired campus on the planet.

When the video ends, the camera-toting crowds disperse for their next destination: Sea World, Universal Studios, another fried lunch. A snow-white couple in matching Goofy visors follows a guide upstairs to see a real estate agent. After the guide returns, I ask him why they want to live in Celebration. Is it the weather? The proximity to Disney World? Space Mountain?

"Nope," he says, blinding me with his smile. "It's the school."

Reinventing Public Education

This isn't the first time technology has been called upon to reinvent public education. Seventy years ago, Thomas Edison predicted movies would eliminate books from the classroom. Later, filmstrips and language labs were supposed to usher in a bold new era of learning. But to many educators, computers aren't just the latest toy, they're a necessity. New Jersey lawmakers, for instance, axed part of their state's school-aid budget to lay out $10 million for PCs [personal computers]. A Boston-area school opted to spend nearly $350,000 on digital gizmos instead of hiring art teachers. And although California schools are still reeling from years of budget cuts, the state has proposed $11 billion for computerizing classrooms.

More programs such as these are on the way. President Bill Clinton has mapped out a $100 billion computer initiative, and has sanctioned a series of national "Net Days," during which parents and other volunteers help wire schools.

Teachers, for their part, rank computer knowledge as more important than biology, chemistry, and history. Proponents say the advantages are clear. Kids in Whitefish, Montana, will be able to comb King Tut's tomb from their desks. Biology students from Tampa and Taiwan will mingle online while they dissect fetal pigs with Smithsonian scientists. The days of mind-numbing drills and sleepy-time lectures will be over. Plus, high-school graduates will be primed to surf the increasingly digital workplace.

Certain issues get lost in all this technobabble. Technological literacy today means mastering basic tasks such as word processing, which is as easy as playing Tetris [a computer game]. And with no solid proof computers boost students' learning, the high cost of maintaining and upgrading a gaggle of laptops, scanners, and CD-ROMs may not be worth the payoff.

Undaunted, Celebration is going full-baud ahead. To hear Larry Rosen tell it, the school is all about "greater freedom" and "flexibility in learning." While no one is saying schools like Celebration's *shouldn't* go digital, some scholars think it's a question of degree. "Celebration is trying to create a model school all at once," says Larry Cuban, Stanford education professor and author of *Teachers and Machines: The Classroom Use of Technology Since 1920.* "There is a long history of efforts to try to do that, some of which have succeeded, but most of which have been damaged or failed."

Educational Fantasia

If Celebration is Disney's educational fantasia, Scott Muri wears the wizard hat. A congenial Southerner with a fat caterpillar mustache, he was working as a science and math teacher in North Carolina when he was recruited to oversee Celebration's technology program. His official title is Instructional Technology Specialist. As he says, "I didn't want to be the fix-it guy."

Muri takes me on a brief campus tour, pointing out that Celebration is still in its Beta phase. The school, initially located in a temporary trailer, has recently moved into its permanent facility outside the town square.

Here, 900 students, a number of whom are from the surrounding county and entered a lottery to gain admission, skip through the building's Froot Loops-colored building and plug in.

"See that kid over there making a poster on the floor?" Muri says as we pass an art class strewn with Nirvana-patched backpacks. "We have software programs and printers that can make this kind of work! See those kids reading those books over there? They could be reading that on the Net or a CD-ROM! See that teacher looking at that student's work on a piece of paper? She'll be looking at it online!"

Soon, Muri says, Celebration will go paperless. That's

right, no more textbooks. Already, students have access to an "electric library" of millions of magazines and books, as well as a media retrieval system that can feed videos or laser discs right to their desktops. Kids can plug laptops to any of the 1,800 data ports socketed throughout the building. They can even get satellite TV.

Jim Borgman. Reprinted by special permission of King Features Syndicate.

It's all part of the school's motto, which Muri describes as "Anytime, anyplace." To milk the intranet [a network that links computers within a business—or community—together] that connects the school to the community, Celebration is creating "electronic portfolios," which will be digital capsules of each student's work. If, while withdrawing cash at an ATM on Main Street, a sophomore suddenly remembers the answer to a homework question on the Hundred Years' War he can simply run over to the bank's computer kiosk, call up the file, and punch it in. The thought of doing Western Civ at the Gap is creepy enough, but parents can also use the portfolios to keep tabs on Junior's progress. In the old days, a student could tell Mom and Dad the dog ate the report card. At Celebration, Rover will have to eat the hard drive.

When Kids Know More than Teachers

As we enter an elementary classroom, where a teacher scurries between kids in various states of spontaneous combustion, I can't help but wonder about the mundane realities that underlie Celebration's vision quest. For the school to become paperless, someone will have to individually scan all the bean collages, algebra quizzes, and hand-written *The Catcher in the Rye* book reports into the network. Who's going to have time to do this? Muri points to a six-year-old boy in the corner, who's struggling to scrawl his name on a wide-ruled sheet of paper. "Him," he says.

The kids don't have much choice if the teachers don't know how to use the machines. I head into the frenetic junior-high section of Upper 3, a Celebration neighborhood that groups kids of different ages into one sprawling class. Teacher Jackie Flanigan looks excited but distraught. Her class is about to boot up for a distance-learning program, a crown jewel of high-tech education that aims to connect students who would otherwise never meet. Clusters of giddy Celebrationeers are huddled around blinking computers, chatting with Indiana farm kids. The assignment is ambitious: to compare cultures and discuss the concept of civilization. For now, though, the topics are more like Saturday afternoon on AOL: skating, a cute chick named Mandy, and Pride, Celebration's new mascot, which, according to two gum-snapping girls, looks like a way-lame mutation of the Lion King with wings.

While the kids gossip and high-five, a freckled girl calls out, "Mrs. Flanigan! Someone's deleting my files!" Mrs. Flanigan emits a volcanic sigh. Clearly, it's enough of a challenge to keep 30 electrified teens on task, let alone save them from getting their data hacked. "I'm not prepared," she tells me in her Holly Hunter drawl. "There aren't many people who *are*, unless you're Bill Gates."

Flanigan isn't alone. According to a recent study, only 15 percent of teachers have had more than nine hours of training in educational technology; 18 states (including Florida) don't even *require* training for a teacher to be certified. The result is a nation full of Jackie Flanigans: thoughtful, dedicated, overworked teachers who don't get the support they need to exploit the pricey tech schools are banking on.

So when the girl panics, it's not Mrs. Flanigan to the rescue, it's a student like Louis Grasso—one of the self-taught techie kids who keep Celebration's computers running. A 17-year-old with an enviable collection of Metallica T-shirts, Louis likes to hack around; he wants a career in computer security systems. There's only one problem. "I barely get my school-work done," he says, "because I'm always fixing computers."

What students like Louis might be losing in class time, they're gaining in status. Introducing computers to a school creates a fundamental shift in the student/teacher relation-ship. Students don't just *think* they're smarter than their teachers, they know it. For administrators, the big concern is how kids will use their new power. Most schools and cor-porations engage in some form of online monitoring. Be-cause so much of Celebration exists online, they've had to take monitoring—eavesdropping, basically—to a unique next step, one Muri affectionately calls "network discipline."

One afternoon, a 15-year-old blader named Steven Kacz-marczyk made the mistake of trash-talking online in the stu-dent chat room. "I basically called one of my friends an ass-hole," Steven says. "Then I insulted his mother." The next day, he was paid a visit by Muri, who waved a printout of the chat-room discussion at Steven and reminded him he could be expelled. Instead, Steven received a more 21st century punishment: He had his computer access suspended. Of course, when Celebration bans a kid's access, it's essentially banning him from the library, the classes, and his homework.

For Steven, whom Flanigan considers one of her bright-est students, there's a not-so-subtle subtext to Celebration's dictum of freedom through technology. "We're paranoid whenever we go on those computers," he says. "It's like someone's always watching you."

Fresh Air and eMates

There are some things a computer can't replicate, like fresh air. I trail along with a science class heading off into the woods a few hundred yards from campus. Snow egrets cut through the sky. This is Florida at its most serene. Deep in the palms, something starts beeping.

At first, Mr. Braley, the group's teacher, doesn't hear a thing. "All right," he says, enthusiastically gutting a plant from the dead brown fronds, "can anyone identify this? Anyone?"

A baggy-jeansed dude says, "Uh, weeds?" But that's the only response. The seven other students are anxiously trying to find the source of the incongruous electronic beeps, which, they suspect, are coming from their eMates: green-shelled, GI Joe-style laptops they brought to take notes on. So far, most of them have been pounding away on their keyboards. Mr. Braley tells me they'd never take so much down if they were using paper and pens. "Maybe it's just the coolness of it," he says.

At this moment, someone seems to be using them for a more recreational purpose. "Yo, check it out," shouts a guy in a Fila shirt and zebra-striped shorts, "it says someone's 'beaming' me! How are they doing that?"

"There's, like, an infrared thingie back here," Louis the hacker explains, "and that, like, beams your notes and shit to whoever else is around." Mr. Braley steps over and asks what's going on.

"Everyone's beaming each other," a pale girl says.

"All right, class," Mr. Braley snaps, "no more beaming!"

The Internet Promotes Passivity

What exactly is being taught using computers? On the surface, pupils learn to read, type and use programs. I'll bet that they're really learning something else. How to stare at a monitor for hours on end. To accept what a machine says without arguing. That the world is a passive, preprogrammed place, where you need only click the mouse to get the right answer. That relationships—developed over E-mail—are transitory and shallow. That discipline isn't necessary when you can zap frustrations with a keystroke. That legible hand-writing, grammar, analytic thought and human dealings don't matter.

Clifford Stoll, *New York Times*, May 19, 1996.

The students clamp shut their eMates, then complain about the bugs. There's a bad virus of encephalitis going around, a pretty blond says, and if she gets bit by a mosquito, her brain will swell up until she dies. Mr. Braley says they'll head back as soon as someone IDs the clump of vegetation.

He hands it to Louis, who, after a few hapless yanks, just shrugs. He doesn't know the answer, and, in Celebration's big scheme, he doesn't really have to. Here, it's more important for kids to be up on what's inside their hard drive than what's outside their window.

Finally, Mr. Braley offers a few hints: The plant is nicknamed for how it feels; it's the same name of the stuff that connects the school and the town; it's something you should be familiar with, Louis. It's called wire.

Books in the Shadows

The next day I polish off a few soggy grilled-cheese sandwiches in the cafeteria, then follow a couple of kids over to the library, or as it's now called, "the media center." Before it was constructed, Paul Kraft, Celebration's information technology specialist, formerly known as librarian, had high hopes: "I envision the walls eventually covered with stimulating material of educational value and kid appeal," he said. "Kind of like in a Hard Rock Cafe or Planet Hollywood."

When I arrive, alas, there are no Keith Moon drumsticks on the wall. In fact, it looks like an ordinary school library with one exception: I don't see any books, just a couple dozen computers clustered the middle of the room, which resembles NASA mission control. A chubby Indian boy starts demoing his latest Web site for me. "It's kind of boring right now," he says, as his name sparkles across the screen, "but I'm working on some cool Java applets that should make it rock."

What doesn't seem to be rocking are the rows of books stacked rather forlornly in the back shadows. The aisles are empty of kids and, according to Kraft, that's how they usually remain. When I ask a couple of students at the computers if they ever consider researching offline, they crack up. "Only when the computers are down," says a skinny 15-year-old boy. The girl next to him agrees: "Yeah, information is definitely better online." With wide eyes, she tells me how she just found an entire Web site devoted to her next research topic: the history of volleyball.

"What if you had to do a report on, say, James Joyce?" I ask.

"Is that spelled with an 'i' or a 'y'?" the boy asks, as he

works his mouse with the precision of a Japanese chef. "Yahoo doesn't spell-check." With a few clicks, he finds a Joyce Web site and, after a quick glance to make sure it has enough text, saves it to his disc. Done deal. I wonder, though, where this info comes from. The boy says he never really checks. When we click the link at the bottom, does it lead to Princeton? Yale? No, it's "Ron's Toga Party!"—a site with a photo collage of Elvis, Santa Claus, and a tongue-wagging drunk who, I presume, is Ron. It seems Ron has a penchant for frat-boy antics, and, of course, Irish modernists.

I have a good laugh with the kids, but would their parents? I ask the boy his name.

"Rosen," he says.

"Is your father Larry, the one who helped set up the school?"

"Yep."

And it turns out the girl is the daughter of Jackie Flanigan, the distance-learning teacher. I feel like I need to reboot. If the bigwigs' kids can't tell James Joyce from Carrot Top, who can? But Celebration isn't about thoughtfulness, it's about speed—the speed to get information, to get schools wired, kids connected, a proverbial bridge to the 21st century. What happens after that seems almost beside the point.

"Hey," I say to Flanigan, "so why do you think this information is better online, anyway?"

"Because," she says, like I'm being really silly, "it's quicker."

"Online self-help groups help people maintain their health, speed recovery and boost their odds of improvement."

Internet Self-Help Groups Can Improve Health Care

Lynne Lamberg

In the following viewpoint, Lynne Lamberg contends that online discussion groups can improve health care by enabling people with medical problems to get help from others suffering similar problems. She contends that the anonymity of cyberspace encourages people with physical disabilities to discuss their problems openly, and because cyberspace is not restricted by geography, sufferers are able to get feedback from diverse people. According to Lamberg, studies show that people who use the Internet to discuss health problems with others tend to get medical help earlier and recover from their illnesses faster. Lynne Lamberg is an independent medical journalist and editor.

As you read, consider the following questions:
1. According to former Surgeon General C. Everett Koop, how can online self-help groups reduce medical costs?
2. How are electronic support groups different from advice columns or radio call-in shows, according to Lamberg?
3. According to the author, what conditions generate the most messages on American Online?

Reprinted, with permission, from Lynne Lamberg, "Patients Go Online for Support," *American Medical News*, April 1, 1996.

"My neurologist acts like my pain is not real," Pat tells others in her multiple sclerosis support group at CompuServe. "I wish he could spend an hour inside my skin."

"My husband has nine of 11 symptoms of depression on a checklist I saw in a magazine," writes Greta at America Online. "He refuses to go to a doctor, and I'm worried sick."

"My doctor says my PSA is too high," reports Bill at Prodigy, giving his test results. "Do I really need a biopsy? Does that hurt?"

Such notes appear by the thousands on electronic support group message boards, among the most visited sites in Cyberspace. From AIDS, Alzheimer's carers, alopecia and autism to weight control and widows/widowers, more than 1,000 online groups already exist, and new ones form every day.

Physicians may find these services a useful adjunct to their care, much like face-to-face support groups in the community, which give participants both practical information and the comforting realization that they are not alone in facing their disease or disability.

Self-help—sometimes called mutual help—groups also may help people maintain their health, speed recovery and boost their odds of improvement, according to studies done in the 1990s of patients with breast cancer, asthma, diabetes, arthritis and other diseases. Medical care costs may be reduced, too, former U.S. Surgeon General C. Everett Koop, MD, has suggested, because patients in self-help groups bring problems to their physicians in an earlier stage and visit emergency departments less often.

Some physicians participate in support-group discussions, answering questions on behalf of various organizations or drug companies, or acting as ad hoc advisers. Many physicians simply look on or "lurk" (not a pejorative term), to gain insight about patients' concerns.

How Groups Work

Patients often come together because they share similar symptoms and problems well before their illness is named and legitimized, said Ed Madara, who directs the American

Self-Help Clearinghouse in Denville, N.J. Gulf-war syndrome and carpal tunnel injuries are conditions that gained public recognition from such networking. "If AIDS had appeared 10 years later, after use of the Internet took off," Madara mused, "preventive efforts might have been better organized and more successful."

Electronic support groups in many ways resemble barn raisings popular in America's frontier days. "It's no coincidence that as traditional supports—family and neighborhood—are fading away, self-help networks are growing rapidly," said Tom Ferguson, MD, senior research associate at Harvard Medical School's Center for Clinical Computing. People who initially go on-line as help seekers often turn into help providers, sharing experiences with newcomers.

Compared with community groups, on-line groups vastly expand opportunities for participation, particularly for people with disabilities and rare disorders. You don't have to be able to see or to type to participate, thanks to voice synthesizers and other devices. There are on-line groups for people with lung transplants, facial disfigurement, stuttering, incontinence, brain tumors and those who are "far from average height." It's common to see notes saying, "I've never talked before to anyone else with ankylosing spondylitis or arthrogryposis multiplex congenita."

"A disability may be very isolating" observed David Manning, EdD, leader of CompuServe's disabilities forum and director of the mainstream center at the Clarke School for the Deaf in Northampton, Mass. "On-line groups," Dr. Manning said, "can beat back the walls of this isolation." Leaders of CompuServe groups for people who are deaf, blind or mobility impaired, or have epilepsy, are similarly affected, and serve as role models for members.

On-line support is a boon to those who lack transportation, fear going out or live in remote areas. For people dealing with sensitive issues such as incest or mental illness, anonymity increases feelings of safety. Unlike most face-to-face groups, on-line groups embrace people of all ages. Madara observes "on-line services also can easily reach out and support family members who are often the 'hidden patients.'"

One can read or post messages at any time. Late evening

hours—roughly 9 P.M. to 2 A.M.—are most popular. Most people write messages off-line, giving time to organize their thoughts and express them more clearly than they might when chatting in person or on the phone. This gives many on-line support-group discussions a "meaty" feel.

An Unprecedented Boon

On-line discussion and support groups let patients and professionals swap experiences and share ideas in ways never before possible.

As a source of knowledge, a sounding board, and a starting point for negotiation in the examining room, the Internet may be an unprecedented boon to both patient and doctor.

Lisa Prevost, *Civilization*, June/July 1999.

Many of the criteria people ordinarily use to form opinions about others—and on which they are judged themselves—disappear on-line. Skin color, sex, manner of dress, weight, occupation, speech impediments, use of a wheelchair—none is apparent. People may use initials, first names, or assumed names, some flamboyant. Or as a dog, sitting at a computer, tells another dog in a *New Yorker* cartoon, "On the Internet, nobody knows you're a dog."

Electronic support groups differ qualitatively from advice columns in the newspaper or radio call-in shows, where the individual's needs are subordinate to entertainment, says Ronald Shellow, MD, clinical professor of psychiatry at the University of Miami School of Medicine and an authority on group psychotherapy. "People who are on-line want to be there and they want to be helpful," he said. "While negative behavior gets more attention in newspapers and on TV, people [on-line] basically are helpful to each other."

Chronic medical problems, particularly those prompting intense emotional issues, generate the most messages at AOL, reports Allen Douma, MD, medical director for Health ResponseAbility Systems, in Herndon, Va., which developed and runs AOL's health and medical forum. While about 1,000 messages are posted each day in this forum, writers represent only a small fraction of readers: 1.4 million people enter the health area each month. Some 40,000 to

50,000 AOL members are physicians, Dr. Douma said. Some groups, such as Alcoholics Anonymous, convene regularly in real time at AOL, CompuServe and Prodigy—the big three—and other commercial services.

Support groups often maintain on-line libraries, where members can both contribute and download information. CompuServe's disabilities forum library, for example, includes a sign language dictionary, a sample letter on the need for better Medicare supplemental insurance, facts on exercise and spasm control, and guidelines for selecting a wheelchair. Many disease-related organizations, such as the American Cancer Society and American Lung Assn., maintain an on-line presence, offering publications and other patient information resources, but the patient support groups operate independently.

On-line Help Moves Off-Line

On-line relationships sometimes inspire real life encounters. One now legendary tale involves a woman with cancer who posted her obituary on The Well, a San Francisco on-line service. Her support group sprang into action, providing meals and doing chores. The event also stimulated on-line discussion of relationships and death and dying.

In another case, a physician found his history of substance abuse aired in his local newspaper. He bought a gun and was considering suicide. Other doctors in his on-line recovery group teamed up to be available to him by phone every hour, all night.

As of this writing, there was no on-line group for impaired physicians.

*"Although electronic communication offers
the capability to deliver better and faster
treatment, . . . the caliber of care has been
sacrificed, and with it the health and
welfare of the consumer."*

Medical Information on the Internet Undermines Health Care

Public Citizen Health Research Group

The Public Citizen Health Research Group is an organization that attempts to give consumers more control over decisions that affect their health. In the following viewpoint, the organization contends that much of the medical information on the Internet is wrong or misleading. For example, a 1997 study found that online information about fever in children was unreliable and, in some cases, put children at risk. The organization reports that some websites recommended the use of aspirin to treat fevers in spite of the fact that current medical guidelines recommend that aspirin never be used in treating fever in children as it has been linked to the often fatal Reye's syndrome disease.

As you read, consider the following questions:
1. Why does the Public Citizen Health Research Group criticize many of the websites' recommendations about the use of acetaminophen in treating fever in children?
2. According to the organization, why should parents be cautious about using ibuprofen as a treatment for fever?

Reprinted, with permission, from "Health Risks of the Internet," by Public Citizen Health Research Group, *Health Letter*, September 1997. Subscriptions are $18/year from Public Citizen Health Research Group, Health Letter, 1600 20th St. NW, Washington, DC 20009 or call (202) 588-1000.

With the advent of the Internet, the medical community has been heralding this new technology as the latest panacea for health care, but reality is a lot closer to Pandora's box. Although electronic communication offers the capability to deliver better and faster treatment, in the haste to maximize this potential, the caliber of care has been sacrificed, and with it the health and welfare of the consumer.

Study Highlights Unreliable Information

In an article published by the *British Medical Journal* (June 28, 1997) researchers assessed the reliability of health care information on the world wide web. Focusing exclusively on fever in children, the researchers conducted a systematic search of parent-oriented web pages using two search engines, Yahoo and Excite. They selected fever because it is both a frequent and usually benign condition that can often be successfully treated without a physician's intervention. Accurate and accessible information would not only reduce parental anxiety, but would also optimize the delivery of care by decreasing the number of unnecessary phone calls to doctors.

Each of the 41 web pages identified, developed by either commercial or non-commercial ventures (individual practitioners, clinics, academic institutions, or other organizations), was compared to the guidelines recommended in a standard medical work, *Fever in Pediatric Practice*, by El-Radhi and Carroll. Specifically, the researchers rated the minimum temperature considered as fever, optimal sites for measuring temperature, pharmacological and physical treatments of fever, and the conditions under which a visit to the doctor is warranted. Only four web pages adhered closely to the main recommendations of the guidelines for this illness. And, according to the study, several of the sites suggested treatments known to place a child at high risk of coma or death without warning of this risk.

Diagnosis

Twenty-six of the pages indicated the optimal site for measuring a child's fever and 28 mentioned a specific temperature at which a child is considered feverish. Although the guide recommends taking a child's temperature in the armpit, more than half (24) suggested the rectal method and only nine of these described the proper procedure involved. Because the temperature necessitating treatment and the best method for assessing fever are somewhat arbitrary, the specific responses to these issues are less critical than the complete absence of their mention. Proper treatment of an illness cannot be managed without first clearly identifying the symptoms. To assume consumers can knowledgeably diagnose without assistance is erroneous.

Treatment

As for therapeutic counseling, the majority (34) of sites refer to drug treatment and nearly all of these (31) recommend acetaminophen (as in Tylenol) as supported by El-Radhi and Carroll. Only eight of these, however, suggest the appropriate dose, some with less frequent intervals than the advocated four hours. This may also pose a problem: the researchers note that underdosing is a more common occurrence than overdosing and can lead to ineffective management of the fever.

While 22 pages actively discouraged the use of aspirin, given the possible association of Reye's syndrome in children with viral infection, three recommended it. As reported in past *Health Letters*, Reye's syndrome is a rare but often fatal disease, commonly found in young children with viral infections and characterized by recurrent vomiting that can lead to coma and death. Aspirin should *never* be administered to treat fever in young children or adolescents.

The suggestion in 14 pages of ibuprofen as an appropriate treatment should also be supported with caution. Although clinical studies have indicated that ibuprofen is at least as effective as acetaminophen, and can be more convenient to administer given the less frequent doses, it is more costly and adverse effects such as stomach upset, bleeding in the gastrointestinal tract and reduced blood flow to the kidneys are more common.

With regard to non-pharmaceutical treatments, 38 sites frequently cited therapies such as increasing the intake of fluids, tepid sponging, and dressing lightly. Of the 22 documents that mentioned tepid sponging, seven also specified a

Criteria for Evaluating Electronic Medical Information

• Authorship: Authors and contributors, their affiliations, and relevant credentials should be provided.

• Attribution: References and sources for all content should be listed clearly, and all relevant copyright information noted.

• Disclosure: Web site "ownership" should be prominently and fully disclosed, as should any sponsorship, advertising, underwriting, commercial funding arrangements or support, or potential conflicts of interest. This includes arrangements in which links to other sites are posted as a result of financial considerations. Similar standards should hold in discussion forums.

• Currency: Dates that content was posted and updated should be indicated.

Jama, April 16, 1997.

---

body temperature above which to initiate the remedy, several of which fell below the standard recommendation of 104–105 degrees Fahrenheit. Sponging is recommended in only occasional cases of very high temperature; this is rarely necessary as the fever-reducing drugs are at least as effective, simpler to use, and cause less discomfort to the child. Only six pages noted the importance of administering a fever-reducing drug *before* sponging, a requirement that needs to be more strongly emphasized. Two pages recommended either cold sponging or sponging with alcohol, both of which are widely discouraged as either counterproductive or directly harmful to the child. Cold sponging leads to shivering which actually raises body temperature and breathing alcohol while being bathed can lead to hypoglycemia (low blood sugar) and coma.

Thirty-six pages also discussed conditions that required a physician's care. Twenty-seven specifically listed warning signs: convulsions, difficulty breathing, stiff neck, and difficulty awakening as warranting a visit to the doctor. Not commonly mentioned were pain, vomiting, headache, earache, delirium, or underlying disease, symptoms also of concern. The guide encourages calling a doctor whenever the child is less than six months old, but only half (21) of the pages include this information and some incorrectly suggest contacting a physician only if the child is as young as two or three months.

The Internet contains a wealth of health-related information, but this research clearly shows that using these types of web pages to diagnose and treat illnesses is like playing Russian roulette.

Periodical Bibliography

The following articles have been selected to supplement the diverse views presented in this chapter. Addresses are provided for periodicals not indexed in the *Readers' Guide to Periodical Literature*, the *Alternative Press Index*, the *Social Sciences Index*, or the *Index to Legal Periodicals and Books*.

Kim Alexander	"It's the Net, Stupid!" *Wired*, November 1998. Available from 520 Third St., 4th Floor, San Francisco, CA 94107.
S.A. Booth	"Essential Technology Guide: Education," *Popular Science*, September 1996.
Claire Ponasian Dunavan	"Web Surfing May Fuel Self-Diagnoses," *Los Angeles Times*, September 25, 2000. Available from Times Mirror Square, Los Angeles, CA 90053.
Pete Du Pont	"The Art of Cyberpolitics," *World & I*, January 1998. Available from 3600 New York Ave. NE, Washington, DC 20002.
Lisa Guernsey	"Education: Web's New Come-On," *New York Times*, March 16, 2000.
Peter J. Leitner	"The Doctor Will 'Virtually' See You Now," *World & I*, July 2000.
Timothy W. Maier	"Should the Mouse Cast Your Vote?" *Insight*, August 28, 2000. Available from 3600 New York Ave. NE, Washington, DC 20002.
George Melloan	"Of the Internet, Civil Society and How They Mesh," *Wall Street Journal*, January 11, 2000.
Michael Pollak	"Searching the Web as a Matter of Life and Death," *New York Times*, June 1, 2000.
Clifford Stoll	"Invest in Humanware," *New York Times*, May 19, 1996.
Leslie Wayne	"On Web, Voters Reinvent Grass-Roots Activism," *New York Times*, May 21, 2000.

CHAPTER 3

Should the Internet Be Regulated?

Chapter Preface

"Firewall" software designed to keep hackers out of computer systems did not stop them from breaking into a network in February 1996 belonging to the Los Alamos National Laboratory, which developed the atomic bomb. In February 2000, hackers bombarded the E*Trade brokerage website with data, which overloaded its system and blocked thousands of investors from accessing its site. Political activists Ricardo Dominguez and Stefan Wray routinely recruit computer programmers to attack the websites of any entities that they deem responsible for oppression. Indeed, malicious hackers can attack with virtual impunity because there is no centralized agency overseeing the Internet to organize a defense against them.

Those concerned about hackers often disagree about how to stop them. Many analysts argue that the government must mandate that Internet service providers set up procedures that will make it easier to identify attackers, perhaps making anonymous correspondence illegal. Writer David Johnson argues that "to achieve a civilized form of cyberspace, we have to limit the use of anonymous communications." Advocates of legislation to curb online anonymity claim that if all users were required to identify themselves, those tampering with networks could be traced and prosecuted.

Many experts, however, argue that government regulation such as anonymity legislation would infringe on the rights of citizens. Attorney Jonathan D. Wallace contends that "legislation against anonymity threatens to end that rich tradition [of free speech in the United States] and should be opposed." Many analysts assert that the Internet needs to remain unfettered by government regulation in order to grow, and claim that the computer industry can create commercial solutions to the hacker problem.

Experts disagree about the extent to which government should become involved in implementing solutions to problems caused by hackers. The authors in the following chapter debate some of the more contentious issues surrounding regulation of the Internet. Until people feel safe online, the debate about how to ensure Internet security will continue.

"Without a minimal set of legally enforceable standards, there is no guarantee that e-commerce outlaws won't overwhelm the guys in the white hats."

Internet Privacy Should Be Protected

Rutt Bridges

In the following viewpoint, Rutt Bridges contends that personal data-collecting by Internet merchants should be regulated. According to Bridges, current law allows online merchants to deposit "bugs" or "cookies" on consumers' hard drives that can track customers' movements through cyberspace and obtain personal information about them. In addition, Bridges maintains that online merchants frequently sell the personal data they collect to other companies, which infringes on consumers' right to privacy. Rutt Bridges writes for the *Denver Rocky Mountain News*.

As you read, consider the following questions:
1. In what specific ways do Web bugs invade a user's privacy, according to Bridges?
2. According to the author, to whom do merchants sell personal data?
3. What is one of the fears that users searching for disease-related information might have about personal profiling, in the author's opinion?

Reprinted from "Internet's Dirty Little Secret: If You Travel the Information Superhighway, You're Probably Being Tailed," by Rutt Bridges, *Denver Rocky Mountain News*, June 24, 2000, by permission of the *Denver Rocky Mountain News*.

111

I magine this: As you enter a store, you are greeted by an expert personal shopping assistant. The assistant knows your individual tastes and accompanies you from department to department, answering questions and making helpful suggestions.

It's almost like the old days, when the shopkeeper knew you and treated you as a valued customer!

As you finish making your selections, they are efficiently added to your account. You leave the store, feeling completely satisfied with your shopping experience.

But when you walk away, you notice something odd:

Your personal shopping assistant has slipped out of the store and is discreetly following you down the street. As you step into a drug store to pick up a prescription, the assistant covertly trails behind, jotting notes. You again notice the assistant watching and writing while you browse through the magazine rack.

As you drive away, the assistant notes the make, model and license plate number of your car. Worse still, the shopping assistant has secretly planted a bug that tracks your every movement! Sound incredible? Welcome to the brave new world of the worst of cyber shopping. The Internet's dirty little secret is the "Web bug" and its sometime accomplice, the "surveillance cookie."

Most people surf the Web under the illusion that no one will ever know what they look at. Not true. Some Web sites can secretly deposit Web bugs on your hard disk to record subsequent sites that you visit. Web bugs can also be used to uncover your personally identifiable e-mail address—and then link it to information the Web bug collects about your browsing habits. One unpleasant result can be an avalanche of junk e-mail.

Web bugs can even be used to track on-line newsgroup discussions where people reveal their views about everything from religion to politics.

If this invasion of privacy concerns you, that's tough. Under current law, there's little you can do about it.

In their most effective and obnoxious form, Web bugs work together with cookies, the tiny files that are placed on your hard disk when you visit most Web sites.

Not all cookies are bad. In fact, cookies can be quite beneficial, adapting to your Web browser and your computer's graphics to enhance your Internet experience. Unfortunately, Web browsers can't tell the high-tech cookie equivalent of mom's delicious chewy chocolate chips from Aunt Edna's rhubarb granola surprise.

Most Web Sites Collect Personal Information

The vast majority of Web sites collect personal information from on-line consumers, and most collect several types of information, such as name, address, Social Security number and birth date.

Percent of Web Sites Collecting Personal Information

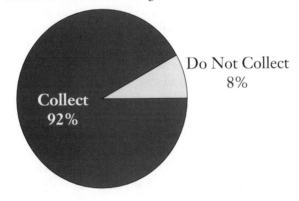

"Privacy Online: A Report to Congress," Federal Trade Commission, June 1998.

Most Web browsers let you automatically refuse all cookies. But cookies are so widely used that blocking them severely limits your browsing experience.

Many consumers don't mind (or know, for that matter) when merchants use cookies as an internal mechanism to track what their customers buy, so they can offer related products in a non-intrusive way. But consumers become much less happy when Web sites sell personal data to spammers, junk mailers and telemarketers, or share such information with other Web sites.

At the bottom of Web pages you often find, in tiny letters,

the word "privacy." By clicking on this link you can view the merchant' s privacy policy.

Be prepared for the legal equivalent of *War and Peace*. One popular Web site uses no fewer than 2,500 words to explain its privacy policy. As Winston Churchill once observed, "The document, by its very length, defends itself against the risk of being read."

Privacy statements usually start with a reassuring promise like "We are committed to safeguarding your privacy on-line." Then they often go on to substantially undermine that promise.

For example, the privacy statement might say that the merchant may "provide" (meaning "sell") information it gathers on you to "trusted partners" (i.e., companies whose checks won't bounce). Finally, the merchant often reserves the right to change this policy at any time and without any notice. But that's OK, since many companies don't strictly adhere to their own privacy policies anyway. Late in this year's legislative session, House Minority Leader Ken Gordon joined forces with House Majority Leader Doug Dean to introduce a remarkable Internet privacy bill that would have become the toughest yet for any state. Many industry observers were shocked that this political "odd couple"— Dean is a Republican from Colorado Springs while Gordon is a Denver Democrat—could get together on such an issue.

In a House Judiciary Committee hearing on the bill, lawmakers learned that Internet marketing companies have developed the ability to track the sites you visit and pop up banner ads relating to your specific interests. This can be beneficial when you are shopping for mountain bikes. However, users are less pleased when their interests are more personal. Internet users surfing for disease-related information have real fears that such personal profiling may find its way into insurance databases. In the end, Dean and Gordon agreed to withdraw the bill and give industry a chance to either propose effective self-regulation or help define acceptable legislation. Clearly, however, public pressure to address privacy concerns will only increase between now and the next legislative session.

Gov. Bill Owens' Commission on Science and Technology recently identified Internet privacy as a key policy issue. At the end of the session, the legislature passed HB 1395, sponsored by Rep. Matt Smith, R-Grand Junction, creating a task force to study all aspects of consumer privacy in Colorado. Hopefully an effective plan of action will emerge from this group.

Students' Privacy at Risk

According to Forrester Research, nearly a quarter of US companies are using information gathered from the Internet to develop detailed profiles of customers. Some are going after the youth market. ZapMe loans computers and a satellite link to schools then collects the names, addresses and phone numbers of students and transfers that information to corporate sponsors.

David Banisar, *Index on Censorship*, March 2000.

Consumer information has always been a valuable commodity in business. In the old days, such information was imprisoned in filing cabinets. But the Internet has revolutionized the ease with which personal information can be harvested and the speed at which it can be shared. Today, the information superhighway is a virtual autobahn; data travels fast and freely, sometimes at great risk to consumers.

Reputable businesses understand the consequences they face if they abuse their customers' trust. But, unfortunately, the Internet has its share of renegades.

It's easy to get most people to agree to not rob each other's homes. But without specific and enforceable laws, a few desperados wreak havoc. Without a minimal set of legally enforceable standards, there is no guarantee that e-commerce outlaws won't overwhelm the guys in the white hats. It would seem reasonable to require companies to inform users of their privacy policies, and to comply with them. It would also seem reasonable to outlaw Web bugs. If anyone can demonstrate a reliable self-regulation model, I will be its greatest champion. But if they can't, it is time for government to step in to protect our personal privacy.

Americans are tired of being watched by machines that never sleep—and never forget.

"Imposing draconian new rules on [Internet] marketing and information sharing would raise costs to consumers, particularly the less affluent."

Internet Privacy Laws Are Unnecessary

Declan McCullagh

Declan McCullagh asserts in the following viewpoint that regulating personal data collecting by online merchants would hinder the growth of Internet commerce, which depends on data collection to make advertising and selling more efficient. He contends that although Internet users say they are concerned about privacy, in reality they voluntarily visit websites that have no privacy protection and freely share personal information. The real danger to privacy comes not from merchants on the Internet, McCullagh claims, but from too much government interference in business and people's personal lives. Declan McCullagh is the Washington bureau chief for *Wired News*, an online news service.

As you read, consider the following questions:
1. What percentage of Americans think there should be new Internet privacy laws, according to McCullagh?
2. In the author's opinion, what alternatives do consumers have if they feel uncomfortable giving personal information to a website?
3. How does personal data collection benefit consumers, according to McCullagh?

Reprinted, with permission, from "Is Internet Privacy Overrated?" by Declan McCullagh, *Liberty*, August 1999.

R obert Pitofsky says he wants to help your children. "Protecting kids who surf the Internet has been a top priority," says the antitrust lawyer-turned-chairman of the Federal Trade Commission (FTC).

Ridiculous Regulatory Schemes

In July 1999 he and the other FTC commissioners laid out a painstakingly detailed 55-page plan that lets the government regulate websites in the name of protecting the public.

One odd result: The scheme robs us of our own privacy in the name of preserving our children's. Parents must hand over personal info like their names and addresses—the idea is to get an adult's OK—before kids can enter websites like Jelly Belly's jellybeans online.

Wacky? Sure. Incoherent? Definitely. Is shielding kids from jelly bean cartoons a good use of the FTC's time? Probably not. But more extreme proposals to regulate the Internet make even Pitofsky's look sensible.

Take Rep. Bruce Vento, (D-MN). His July 1999 Consumer Internet Privacy Protection Act was referred to a House Commerce subcommittee. The legislation says websites may no longer share "personally identifiable information" about their visitors without prior "written consent."

Written consent? We're talking about demanding a paper letter and an envelope and a signature here, folks—a scheme that makes about as much sense as insisting you sign your John Hancock with a quill pen. And, yes, Vento's chronologically-backward bill applies even to Net-savvy adults itching to sign up to physical or electronic mailing lists to receive news, sports scores, or discount offers at their local hardware store. Suffice it to say that the measure is not exactly a boon to electronic commerce.

Privacy Debates Heat Up in Washington

Whether Vento's plan will succeed or not is an open question.[1] But one thing that is certain is that privacy has emerged as one of the hottest topics in Washington, causing legislators to stumble over each other in a bull-headed stam-

1. The Consumer Internet Privacy Protection Act was still being reviewed by the House Commerce Subcommittee at the date of publication.

pede to do something, anything, without considering the long-term consequences.

Public opinion is spurring politicians along. Over a quarter million irate Americans complained about federal bank snooping rules, and new government DNA databases are causing more jitters than a case of Jolt Cola.

Polls showing Americans fret about their privacy seem to echo this concern. One survey found that 81% of Net users are concerned about threats to privacy online. In another, 72.2% of Americans polled said there should be new "Internet privacy laws."

One problem with these polls, though, is that talking abstractly about privacy is a pointless exercise. If you ask would-be car buyers if they value low prices, you'll get general agreement. But if you broaden your query to include safety, fuel efficiency, performance and reliability, you will likely hear that those options easily justify a higher sticker price.

So it is with privacy. The polls do not explain the downside of regulations. Imposing draconian new rules on marketing and information sharing would raise costs to consumers, particularly the less affluent who rely more on free or low-cost services supported by advertising. By hurting startups that would otherwise rent mailing lists, regulation hands established firms an unfair advantage.

Don't get me wrong. It is natural to be a little nervous about privacy. But nobody—except the government—can force you against your will to hand over your personal information online. If you do not feel comfortable giving information to a website, you have got plenty of other options. Do not type it in. Do not go there anymore. Sign up with a service like anonymizer.com. Or lie.

The Economics of Privacy

In a free society, government regulation should be a last resort. Economists generally agree that the government should step in only when the free market has a glaringly obvious problem.

But when it comes to privacy, so-called market failures generally occur when federal bureaucrats and privacy advocates disagree with choices consumers have made. By and large, the bulk of consumers do not care as much about on-line privacy as they claim in polls. Websites without privacy policies have received thousands of e-mail addresses typed in by people hoping to get daily or weekly updates on topics they care about.

More Safeguards on the Net than Off

Despite the Internet's reputation as privacy's gravest modern threat, consumers are increasingly finding more safeguards on the Net than off.

A study released in May 1999 offers new evidence of this trend, showing a sharp rise in the number of websites that post policies telling people what information is collected from them and how it is used.

Nearly two-thirds of the Net's 7,500 most popular commercial sites voluntarily post privacy policies, according to a statistical sampling of those sites by Georgetown University. That compares with 14% that did so in 1998 when a similar survey was conducted by the government.

The survey is the latest illustration of how much attention is being paid to the Internet as a privacy menace, an image cultivated in recent years by government summits, congressional hearings and extensive news coverage.

But often lost amid the hand-wringing is the fact that consumers, even tireless Internet surfers, still shed more exploitable data as they wander through everyday life.

Greg Miller, *Los Angeles Times*, May 13, 1999.

But most large companies do tell you what they will do with information you provide. It should be obvious that the goals of Internet entrepreneurs are pretty simple: To make money, to burnish their firm's reputation, to boost its market valuation. Anything that helps them lure consumers to websites and keep them there will help—and entrepreneurs are smart enough to puzzle out if privacy policies and limits on reselling personal information will be attractive or not. In the Internet economy, stock prices are valued with an eye to future visits and future traffic—and there is no single better way to prevent that from happening than losing your customers' confidence by misusing their personal data.

In other words, more than most businesses, websites are

unusually subject to the supremacy of consumers. Every day, companies are forced to adjust their content and business model so visitors will find their websites alluring. As Austrian economist Ludwig von Mises wrote: "If they fail in these endeavors, they suffer losses and must, if they do not succeed in amending their methods, go out of business." Or at least watch their stock price plummet as a flood of e-mail from angry investors arrives.

Why Privacy Is Overrated

European-style regulations of information collection would have a tremendous negative economic impact. It is no accident that the Internet has flourished the most in the U.S., a country with limited regulation compared to European states, and certainly nothing as invasive as the European Data Directive. European regulators have barred American Airlines, for instance, from transferring customer information from Sweden to its SABRE reservation system in the U.S.

Arguments for intervention aren't supported by either theory or experience. The much-reviled "privacy intrusions" by corporations generally are far from the enemy of the consumer. In many cases, they are essential to providing the zero-cost content Internet users have come to expect. Compiling personal information lets businesses become more efficient and produce only products that people want. It reduces waste—who wants to get tons of glossy catalogs featuring products they care nothing about? It also helps in customization, as anyone who uses my.yahoo.com [an online customized news service] knows.

Don Boudreaux, president of the Foundation for Economic Education, likens customization to a good tailor. "Wealthy people get custom shirts, custom-made shoes, and a lot of custom-made items. They take your measurements and keep your name on file," he says. "What this new technology is doing is making it easier for merchants to give the same benefits of customization that were only available to the wealthy before."

It makes sense, of course, to be suspicious of government collection of information. When the Feds step in, consumers don't have a choice—they get a one-size-fits-all rule. Government plans like the creation of an air traveler profiling system announced in August 1999, and the trend toward larger and larger government databases, should give any thoughtful person cause for concern.

But far too often, government databases you're unwillingly entered into are equated with databases of private-sector companies to which you give information voluntarily. Not helping matters is the fact that the privacy debate has been dominated by an alphabet soup of liberal groups like the American Civil Liberties Union (ACLU), Electronic Privacy Information Center, Computer Professionals for Social Responsibility, Center for Democracy and Technology, Privacy International, and Electronic Freedom Foundation, all of which have busied themselves for the last decade demanding increased government regulation of businesses. Even prominent Republicans have joined the chorus. At the Computers, Freedom and Privacy conference in July 1999 in Washington, Rep. Bob Barr (R-Georgia) said information collection by businesses needed to be regulated. High-tech firms have been unwilling to stand up for their First Amendment rights to gather and share information, rights that privacy regulations often conflict with.

"Nobody has a vested emotional interest in debunking these arguments," says Eugene Volokh, a University of California, Los Angeles law professor specializing in the Internet. "Businesses care about the bottom line, not politics."

Many privacy advocates also are instinctively hostile to high-tech firms. Like early 20th century socialists, they claim the institutions of a market economy can be easily abused by corporate overlords. Recently in an article about [online bookstore] Amazon.com's purchase of Alexa Internet, Evan Hendricks, editor of *Privacy Times*, compared the online bookseller to Big Brother. "They are putting their customers under surveillance," Hendricks said. "Amazon.com customers will be at the mercy of Amazon."

Not quite. Hendricks doesn't seem to have heard about [online bookstore] BarnesandNoble.com.

"Federal investigators and prosecutors can and must bring cases [against Internet pornographers] which would . . . be a giant step towards stopping sexual exploitation."

Laws Regulating Internet Pornography Should Be Enforced

Robert Flores

Robert Flores serves as commissioner on the Congressional Child Online Protection Act Commission. In the following viewpoint, excerpted from testimony delivered to the Congressional Subcommittee on Telecommunications, Trade, and Consumer Protection, he maintains that existing obscenity laws apply to pornography peddled over the Internet and should be enforced. He claims that Internet pornography harms children and families by increasing the incidence of sexual abuse and addiction. The argument that Internet pornography cannot be regulated because much of it originates in other countries is specious, Flores contends, because most porn is made in the United States and is subject to U.S. obscenity laws.

As you read, consider the following questions:
1. How much money does Internet pornography generate, according to Flores?
2. In the author's opinion, what predominant theme is featured in today's adult Internet pornography?
3. What are "push" technologies, according to Flores?

Reprinted from "Obscenity on the Internet," Robert Flores's congressional testimony before the House Subcommittee on Telecommunications, Trade, and Consumer Protection's Oversight Hearing: Obscene Material Available via the Internet, May 23, 2000.

M r. Chairman and Honorable Members of this Committee, thank you for providing me with an opportunity to testify this morning on the important and troubling issue of the explosive and uncontrolled growth of obscenity on the Internet. In my career as an Assistant D.A. in Manhattan, acting Deputy Chief of the Department of Justice's Child Exploitation and Obscenity Section, as a special law enforcement advisor with the National Law Center for Children and Families, and now as a Commissioner on the Congressional Child Online Protection Act (COPA) Commission, I have seen the vicious tactics of the pornography syndicates, the destruction handed out by pedophiles, and the value in effective law enforcement over the years. I believe in the law as an answer to criminal social problems and I know that vigorous and fair enforcement of the law can solve many of those problems when prosecutors use the laws given them by their Legislatures.

Internet Porn: Ubiquitous and Profitable

It is obvious that the uncontrolled growth of this criminal activity must be effectively addressed, and soon, or Congress will continue to be confronted with the need for increased regulation, rising levels of sexual abuse and dysfunction in adults and children, increased health care costs to treat those dysfunctions and the victims of sexual abuse and addiction, the poverty that results from broken homes and marriages over sexual abuse and addiction, and even the slower growth of Internet use by children and families who are rightly afraid of its dark side.

In the past five years, much has changed in the size and nature of the Internet based pornography industry, mostly on the World Wide Web and Usenet newsgroups [in which users share information of mutual interest]. In late 1995, few of the major pornographers had a major presence on the Net. While the amount of material that was then available was astounding by anyone's count, today it is available in quantities and formats that make it a ubiquitous commodity. Today, obscenity merchants have gone public, as in the NASDAQ and other capital markets. *Forbes* reports that "pornography to the tune of $1 billion already flows over the Internet."

In addition to the change in the amount of material on the Internet, a look at what now comprises a sizeable and growing portion of hard-core obscenity should send shivers up the spine of every person of good will. Today, adult pornography sites have moved to feature, as a predominant theme, sexually explicit material which is marketed as depicting "teen," "young," "Lolita," "virgin," and "high school" girls and boys. Once the sole province of child pornographers, this jargon and code has now become a staple of adult obscenity marketers.

Pushing Porn at Children

Does this threaten children? You better believe it does. Our kids and grand-kids see it and become indoctrinated by it. Pedophiles and porn addicts see it and become incited by it. Even the U.S. Supreme Court recognized that the mere existence of child pornography images is an ongoing danger to children, because of the stimulating effect it has on pedophiles and the seductive effect it has on children. That's why Congress criminalized the possession of child pornography . . . and added computerized child porn. . . . How strange indeed, if alone among all other speech, adult obscenity did not also stimulate and encourage people to action.

The pornography industry has also become among the most aggressive marketers on the Internet, using newly developed "push" technologies alongside offensive and fraudulent marketing ploys. Thus, even if it were ever true, and I doubt it, that only those who sought out obscenity could find it, today only a lucky few are able to avoid it, as the Internet user community is bombarded with advertisements, tricked into visiting sites, given hot links to porn when search engines are asked for innocent sites, sent unsolicited porn spam [junk] e-mails, and trapped in endless mousetraps that bounce them from porn site to porn site when they try and leave.

In spite of the explosive growth in the distribution of obscenity, aggressive marketing efforts which assault and trap unwilling Web surfers, and a focus on material which portrays children as a suitable sexual interest for adults, the Department of Justice has refused to take action.

It is critical for the Congress to recognize that this refusal of the Justice Department to enforce existing obscenity laws is unjustified and inexcusable. Members of this Congress and your predecessors have provided the tools and means to address this problem, but those federal statutes are not being used.

The Obscenity Test

The record should be clear that there is no question as to what the test is that will be applied when prosecutions are brought involving Internet distribution or pandering of obscene material. Even in the Communications Decency Act of 1996 and Child Online Protection Act of 1998 cases, cases which are well known to the pornography industry, the Supreme Court and federal District Courts recognized that federal obscenity law, based on the Miller test,[1] applies to the Internet.[2] As the Supreme Court stated in 1997 in *Reno v. ACLU* . . . : "Transmitting obscenity and child pornography, whether via the Internet or other means, is already illegal under federal law for both adults and juveniles." While this is not a point to which some may want to draw attention, that is the law. Moreover, those courts offered enforcement of existing obscenity and child pornography laws as part of the solution to the problem of protecting minors from sexually explicit material. Moreover, the Department of Justice represented to the courts that they would do so, though they have yet to prosecute a single case of substance.

Legal Jurisdiction

Just as the test for obscenity remains the same, the reach and applicability of the criminal prohibitions to Internet distribution and pandering of obscenity also remains the same. Thus, someone who sells obscenity may be prosecuted in the place where he stores the material on his computer, any district through which it passes, and the district into which it is received. . . . It is a felony to use the phone

1. In 1973, the U.S. Supreme Court's decision in *Miller v. California* set the guidelines for determining obscenity. 2. The U.S. Supreme Court ruled in 1997 that the Communications Decency Act was unconstitutional. In 1999, the American Civil Liberties Union won an injunction against the Child Online Protection Act. That legislation was still being reviewed by the courts at press time.

lines and other communications carriers and facilities of interstate and foreign commerce to knowingly upload, download, or transmit obscenity.

In 1996, in order to clarify that federal laws apply to the Internet, Congress . . . specifically included "interactive computer services" among those facilities which may not be used to traffic obscenity. Even then, the Department was unwilling to move forward to address this criminal activity and in four years not a single Internet based obscenity case has been brought by main Justice.

On-Line Red Light Districts

If someone let a child browse freely through an adult bookstore or an X-rated video arcade, I suspect and hope that most people would call the police to arrest that person. Yet these very offenses occur every day in America's electronic neighborhoods. A child can get on the information superhighway and freely ride to on-line "red light districts" that contain some of the most perverse and depraved pornographic material available.

Jim Exon, *Computerworld*, February 19, 1996.

Finally, even the question of foreign transmissions into the United States has been answered and there is no serious debate that we cannot reach conduct which originates in foreign countries. The frequently heard argument that we really can't do anything about Internet obscenity because so much of it comes from overseas is specious. Most of the world's hard-core obscenity comes from America's porn syndicates and they are subject to U.S. law no matter where they send their criminal materials from or to. Hiding their Web servers overseas won't save them, we can still prosecute American criminals in U.S. District Courts and seize their assets and credit card receipts from U.S. banks. Moreover, I can't imagine it could be used by the Justice Department to justify its lack of effort. For in testimony on March 9, 2000, before the Committee on the Judiciary, Deputy Assistant Attorney General Kevin Di Gregory, took justifiable pleasure in announcing that the week before his testimony, "a jury in federal district court in New York found Jay Cohen, owner of an

Internet gambling site in Antigua, guilty of violating . . . a statute that makes it illegal for a betting or wagering business to use a wire communication facility to transmit bets or wagers in interstate or foreign commerce."

Contrary to the complaints made by some, the courts have consistently made clear that federal obscenity law applies in cyberspace as it does in real life. Thus, the answer to the question of who and what may be prosecuted under federal obscenity law is as well known to the American Civil Liberties Union (ACLU) and pornography industry lawyers as it is to Government prosecutors. Title 18 of the U.S. criminal code applies to Internet distribution and pandering and may be used today by prosecutors interested in protecting children and families from this scourge.

America Should Lead by Example

As a practical matter, I believe that federal investigators and prosecutors can and must bring cases which would make a difference for average families and which would be a giant step towards stopping sexual exploitation. For example, prosecutions can be brought against the website owners who most directly profit from this form of human exploitation. The producers and distributors of movies, pictures, and other obscene material who wholesale them to the websites for resale can also be pursued under existing law. The recruiters and procurers of women who run virtual prostitution operations making live images available through the Internet may also be prosecuted for transmitting obscenity. And finally, those who bankroll these operations, many of whom have historically been organized criminal operations, may also be investigated and prosecuted.

Leaders and businesses in Europe, Asia, Latin America, and our other trading partners look to the United States to see what we, the major source of obscenity worldwide, will do with this form of exploitation. In fact, there is a 1911 Treaty on the Suppression of Obscene Publications that would provide an existing framework for international cooperation to deal with hard-core obscenity on the Internet and World Wide Web. That Treaty is still in force and now has at least 126 member countries as signatory nations, including most of the Americas, Europe, and Asia. We seek to lead in every other Internet related area, why not here as well? Can money be made by this industry? Of course. In fact, it is one of the few guaranteed ways to succeed financially on the Internet. But at what cost? It is not free, either to the people who consume the products or the society where it runs rampant. We cannot fail to lead simply on the assumption that some amount of obscenity comes from overseas. To do that would be to turn over our Country and its safety to pornographers and sex business operators who are savvy enough to move their servers and remote offices overseas. We don't do it in any other area of criminal law, why would we start here?

Benevolent Neglect?

Our Constitution protects speech, it does not protect obscenity. The President and the Justice Department in particular must recognize that difference and fulfill their obligation to pursue violations of the laws passed by Congress. Mindlessly investigating and prosecuting cases, whether child pornography, child stalking, or even obscenity, will not make children and adults safe from being assaulted by material that is not only offensive but illegal. A comprehensive and coherent strategy which addresses each of the major aspects of the obscenity and sex business operations is necessary. Whoever is blessed with the opportunity to lead [the country as president beginning in 2001] will bear the responsibility of choosing a path down which we will all walk. It is hard to imagine leadership on this issue being worse than today, when the pornography trade association is able to ask the question in its March 2000 trade publication, "How likely is it, would you say, that we are going to enjoy the same benevolent neglect that the industry has enjoyed under Janet Reno?" It is shameful that the American porn industry has come to look at law enforcement in that way.

Thank you for the opportunity to address this Committee.

> *"The only proper, effective, and realistic force that can keep children from inappropriate materials is the combination of parents and private industry. . . . Legislation is simply wrong and ineffective."*

The Government Should Not Regulate Internet Pornography

Keith Wade

Keith Wade is the director of finance at Cypress Gardens in Florida and an adjunct instructor of business and information technology at Webster University. In the following viewpoint, Wade argues that federal laws intended to keep children from obscene materials on the Internet infringe on the free speech rights of adults. He claims that parental supervision and non-governmental solutions—such as family-friendly websites and filtering software that blocks inappropriate websites—can protect children from online pornography more effectively than government regulation.

As you read, consider the following questions:
1. According to Wade, what is the Communications Decency Act?
2. In the author's opinion, why are most commercial websites uninterested in targeting children?
3. What is MayberryUSA, according to Wade?

Reprinted, with permission, from Keith Wade, "The Internet: Parental Guidance Preferred," *Ideas on Liberty*, February 2000.

It is probably helpful—given how venturing into the areas of "obscene" and "inappropriate" can often lead to name-calling and misunderstanding—to make a point very clear immediately. I do not intend to argue that obscene or otherwise inappropriate materials should exist, that the Internet should be a vehicle for delivering them, or that children should have access to them.

Non-Governmental Solutions

Rather, my point is that the only proper, effective, and realistic force that can keep children from inappropriate materials is the combination of parents and private industry. Although a commonly deployed strategy, legislation is simply wrong and ineffective. (Indeed, the FBI's *A Parent's Guide to Internet Safety* advises parents to "Utilize parental controls provided by your service provider and/or blocking software" and "Monitor your child's access to all types of live electronic communications [chat rooms, instant messages, Internet Relay Chat, etc.], and monitor your child's e-mail.") As will be discussed, we can agree on a proper mechanism for restricting children's access while allowing each household to decide for itself which materials it deems "inappropriate."

There are few among us who believe that children should have unrestricted access to the Internet (or television, movies, books, or the beer and wine aisle at the local grocery store, for that matter). While issues and viewpoints vary, most of us accept that at least some things should be the exclusive purview of adults. The Internet has provided children whose parents do not supervise their activities with access to a goodly number of these things.

Given unfortunate incidents [where children become victims of online predators], there is a redoubled interest in keeping children from inappropriate materials; the government seems more than willing to help. There is, however, simply no need for the government to assist parents in this way. There already exist—in addition to the obvious "no brainer" solution of supervising one's children—ample economic incentives, free or low-priced tools, filtered Web access, private-industry utilities, and not-for-profit service groups to exclude children from "offensive" online material.

The Communications Decency Act

Perhaps one of the most blatant offenses against freedom of speech in this country in the past several decades is the Communications Decency Act of 1995. While the act was declared unconstitutional in 1997, the idea of censoring the Internet is one that will not die.

The act would have made it a crime for anyone to use

> any interactive computer service to display in a manner available to a person under 18 years of age, any comment, request suggestion, proposal, image, or other communication that, in context, depicts or describes, in terms patently offensive as measured by contemporary community standards, sexual or excretory activities or organs, regardless of whether the user of such service placed the call or initiated the communication.

On the surface, many people find no problem with this. Children do not have the same rights as adults, and few would argue that they should have them. There are clear-cut reasons for keeping certain materials away from children until their judgment, values, and sensibilities have matured. But legislation such as this denies access not only to children but also to adults who presumably have every right to decide for themselves what offends them.

"Available to a person under 18 years of age" is an exceedingly broad and terribly subjective term. Does this mean, for example, "available to persons under 18 whose parents do a good job of supervising them" or "available to persons under 18 who are fraudulently misrepresenting themselves (perhaps to assist law-enforcement officers entrap someone)"? Considering that an Internet service provider or website operator cannot look at driver's licenses, the only way to outlaw access by youth is to outlaw "inappropriate" sites entirely. Much as we might like to do that, the Constitution is fairly clear in prohibiting censorship of communication we do not like, even for something as laudable as protecting the nation's children.

Perhaps as big a problem as the unconstitutionality of outlawing "offensive" Internet material is the definition of "offensive." This is an area in which one size simply does not fit all. While children may have to bow to the idol of secular humanism in public schools, parents still have the right to instill whatever values they wish at home. Most parents make an effort to shield their children from bad influences during the impressionable years. These bad influences, however, vary from parent to parent. One person's "family values" is another's "hateful speech." One family's "intolerance" is another family's "fundamental beliefs." I recently received a self-diagnosis book from my HMO that I would never let a child see; one company's "educational materials" are my family's "full frontal nudity" and "simulated sexual activity." Parental values simply vary too widely to let any one group decide what is appropriate for children.

Enter the Free Market

Fortunately, we need not rely on legislation to keep children from sites they ought not see. The free market offers numerous solutions.

Many magazines (the ones behind the counter at the bookstore) have been ruled legal but are deemed inappropriate for children. What stops children from picking up the phone, calling the toll-free number, and getting a subscription (after all, magazines do not require proof of age)? Money. Even if parents don't monitor the incoming mail (probably for the same reason they don't monitor their children's computer usage), children are not known for their dis-

Dwane Powell for *The Raleigh (N.C.) News & Observer*. Reprinted by permission of Dwane Powell and Creators Syndicate, Inc.

cretionary income or access to checks and credit cards.

Few folks operate commercial websites out of the goodness of their hearts. Setting up and running a site costs money. While there may be people who put "offensive material" on the Web just for the sake of doing it, most have products to sell. There's no economic incentive to let kids into the site.

One incentive to keep kids out is the money that age-verification companies will pay site operators to do it. Several companies pay Webmasters a commission for each patron referred for age verification. The patron pays for an access number after proving he's of age, then uses it at restricted sites.

Adult Check, for instance, advertises that it provides Webmasters with protection and profits. The company has developed "a complete system of adult verification, identification number assignment and a lucrative income earning opportunity for Webmasters." Tens of thousands of Webmasters have installed this gatekeeping solution, and numerous verification competitors (each with screens full of information about the potential profit for Webmasters) have popped up.

Family-Friendly Filters

Many companies have entered the market to provide "family friendly" Web surfing. MayberryUSA markets itself as a child-safe Internet service provider (ISP). It offers

> a filtering system designed to give our netizens the best in Internet protection. We check the entire Internet daily, and update our filter. MayberryUSA wishes to provide its members with the best the web can offer and to protect its citizens from the dangers of pornography, hate groups, criminal skills, illegal drugs, and other offensive material.

Realizing that "offensive" means different things to different people, MayberryUSA lets users help define what is accessible to themselves and their children:

> anytime you find an offensive site, YOU can help protect our community. Click the green *Sheriff* sign on our sign post or the *Badge* at the top of any of our main pages and make your report. We will take immediate action to filter that site from the MayberryUSA community.

America Online also permits users to restrict access to AOL areas, Web sites, chat rooms, and instant messaging through its "parental control" feature.

Perhaps the most important thing about family-friendly Web sites and surfing is that they are voluntary (and therefore have a keen interest in staying closely aligned with their customers). If someone does not want or need restrictions, or thinks his provider is letting in too much indecency, or thinks it's gone overboard in its restrictions, he can change providers.

The Impulse to Censor

James Madison warned us that the Bill of Rights was a mere "parchment" and that the cause of freedom lay in the hearts of our citizens. No single Supreme Court decision can permanently guarantee free speech anymore than the First Amendment itself can. Has the battle over censorship of the Internet been won [now that the Communications Decency Act of 1996 has been ruled unconstitutional]? The battle, but not the war. So long as blue-nosed officials and self-appointed moralists claim the power and duty to dictate, on pain of fines and incarceration, what people can read and see, so long as the repressive spirit of Censor Anthony Comstock lives on in the likes of Senators Jesse Helms and Jim Exon, so long as parents abdicate their responsibilities to "Big Brother," the impulse to censor will survive and eternal vigilance will remain the price of liberty.

Stephen F. Rohde, *Gauntlet*, 1997.

For the parents who would prefer not to rely on Webmasters and Internet service providers to prevent access to children, there are many software alternatives. The newest versions of Microsoft Internet Explorer and Netscape Navigator include filtering capabilities that allow parents to decide what can be accessed. In the latest edition of Internet Explorer one can choose from five different categories of violence, from "no violence" to "wanton and gratuitous violence." Sex, nudity, and obscenity screens have similar continuums.

While most legislation aims strictly at pornography, the commercial tools give parents control over much more. The maker of Net Nanny says the product "isn't limited in terms of content type. You can screen and block anything such as Pornography, bomb-making formulas, hate literature . . . or whatever else concerns you. If you can define it, Net Nanny can block it!" Another product, CYBERsitter, "includes databases in numerous categories of web sites you might want to restrict access to."

Online Guardian Angels

There's yet another kind of protection for children in cyberspace. Much as they did on the urban streets, the Guardian Angels, through their CyberAngels branch, help police enforce existing laws regarding child pornography and child abuse in cyberspace. "We're your cyber-neighborhood watch," the organization literature says. "We find and report illegal material online, educate families about online safety and how to enjoy cyberspace together, work with schools and libraries, and share basic Internet tips and help resources." CyberAngels also monitors the Web and furnishes its list of 8,000 offending sites to filter-software companies and family-friendly ISPs.

Further, the group provides a babysitting service:

Our [volunteer] CyberMoms do what moms do best . . . keep their and your kids safe online. Specially trained to spot child predators online, they volunteer to moderate kids' chats and watch children in cyber-playgrounds for online services and websites.

We currently have many laws against the exploitation of children. While society is undoubtedly served when those who prey on children are caught, tried, convicted, and locked up, the damage to the children has already been done by the time offenders are apprehended. The virtue of private-sector methods to keep children away from inappropriate materials and computer users is that they prevent such harm.

One of the great truths in life is that families and private industry can generally do things better and more efficiently than government. This is no less true in cyberspace.

> *"The result [of selling tax-free over the Internet] will be a massive loss of the income state and local governments need to fund schools and other basic and needed services."*

The Government Should Tax Internet Commerce

Byron Dorgan

Current tax laws require that all purchases online be taxed. However, in the following viewpoint, Byron Dorgan argues that these taxes often go unpaid because the collection system is complex and burdensome to both consumers and merchants. He contends that the tax collection system must be simplified so that consumers and online businesses will comply with current laws. Furthermore, Dorgan maintains that enforcing Internet tax laws is the only way to ensure that Main Street businesses—which must collect sales taxes—can compete with Internet businesses, and asserts that such taxes help fund schools, fire departments, and other important public services. Byron Dorgan is chairman of the U.S. Senate Democratic Policy Committee and a member of the Senate Committee on Commerce, Science and Transportation.

As you read, consider the following questions:
1. In Dorgan's opinion, why do existing tax laws governing remote sales put an undue burden on the customer?
2. According to the author, why do existing tax laws governing remote sales pose a significant burden for Internet sellers?
3. What does Wal-Mart intend to do in order to compete with Internet companies, according to Dorgan?

Reprinted from Byron Dorgan, "Rapid Growth of Sales Raises Serious Tax Issues," *The San Diego Union-Tribune*, June 11, 2000.

There is a spirited debate in Congress on the subject of Internet taxation. As the Internet continues to grow at an unprecedented rate and continues to touch each of our lives in more important ways, this debate will affect each of us.

No New Taxes

First, it's important to understand what the Internet tax issue is about and what it is not about.

It is not about taxing access to the Internet and it is not about imposing new taxes on Internet transactions.

Congress already has voted to prohibit state and local governments from enacting new taxes on access to the Internet. We also enacted legislation that prohibits discriminatory tax plans which would apply to the Internet but not other kinds of transactions. These prohibitions make good sense to me. This new technology is becoming a real growth engine for our economy. We ought not to allow governments to impose access or discriminatory taxes in a way that would stunt its growth.

And despite what you may have heard, the ongoing debate in Congress is not about creating any new taxes on sales that occur on the Internet. In most states, sales or use taxes are routinely owed on all remote sales, such as catalogue and Internet sales just as they are owed on the sales that take place on Main Street.

What the debate is about is how to collect those taxes which already are owed state and local governments.

The Current Tax Burden

Collecting a sales tax in a face-to-face transaction on Main Street or at the mall is a relatively simple process. The seller collects the tax and remits it to the state or local government.

But with remote sales—such as catalogue and Internet sales—it's more difficult. States can't require a seller to collect a sales tax unless the business has an actual location or sales people in the state. So most states, and many localities, have laws that require the local buyer to send an equivalent use tax to the state or local government when a sales tax was not collected at the time of purchase.

The reality, however, is that customers almost never do

that. It's an enormous burden for an individual customer to file use tax returns with state and local governments for remote purchases they make from catalogues and over the Internet. So, despite the requirement in the law, most simply don't do it. This tax which is owed, is not paid, because it is such a nuisance to do so.

Not Taxing Internet Sales Could Cost Billions

If the federal government doesn't require Internet commerce to be taxed, consumers may take their business to cyberspace, hurting local merchants and eroding communities' tax bases. The potential loss in tax revenue by 2003 could be 20 percent of current local sales taxes, according to some estimates.

Potential Sales-Tax Losses from Electronic Commerce

States	Total U.S. Sales Tax Revenue 1996 ($Billions)	Potential Tax Loss From 20% Decline ($Billions)
Less-Populated States (< 2 million)	$7.2	$1.4
Populated States (2–4 million)	14.1	2.8
More-Populated States (4–7 million)	29.5	5.9
Most-Populated States (> 7 million)	72.2	14.4

Sources: National League of Cities, National Conference of State Legislatures, National Governors' Association.

Internet and catalogue sellers argue that collecting the tax would be a significant burden for them, as well. They would have to comply with tax laws from thousands of taxing jurisdictions—46 states and thousands of local governments have sales taxes. They would have to deal with different tax rates and all the different choices that states and local governments have made on what is taxable and what is nontaxable. They have a point!

Some remote sellers do not want to collect the tax because, frankly, they have an advantage over Main Street businesses. They can sell a product without collecting the tax, whereas Main Street businesses must collect the local sales tax while making the sale. Main Street businesses claim that is unfair competition. And they have a point, too.

Simplify Tax Collection

It seems to me the solution is to require state and local governments to dramatically simplify things for the remote seller. When they have done that, then we can ask the remote seller to collect the tax, freeing the consumer from the burden of having to report it individually.

If state and local governments want remote sellers to collect the sales or use tax on the transaction, then we should expect them to enact a compact that dramatically simplifies their sales tax laws in two specific ways.

1) Each state must develop one blended tax rate with which all remote sellers can comply. In other words, one tax rate per state.

2) At a minimum, within each state there must be a uniform tax base on which remote sellers apply the tax, as well as a uniform list of exempt items.

If there is a single rate and a simplified tax base, I believe the states will have dramatically eased the burden for Internet or catalogue sellers to collect the tax. Congress should then allow state and local governments to collect the tax that is owed at the point of sale.

Important Local Revenue

This issue is important to state and local governments because as the growth of the Internet and catalogue sales accelerates there will be a dramatic reduction in sales tax collections that are used to build and maintain our schools, roads, and police departments. These taxes provide the revenue local governments must rely on to provide for their education, transportation, and public safety needs. State and local governments know that if this matter isn't resolved, they will soon find the revenue sources they rely on to fund these important activities drying up.

Testimony at a congressional hearing in 2000 makes clear just how real that possibility is becoming.

A representative of Walmart told us that it is separately incorporating a business to put Walmart on the Internet. Walmart intends to do so in a manner that will allow it to be exempt from collecting sales taxes when items are sold over the Internet. The reason? Even though Walmart has locations in every state and would therefore be required to collect sales taxes on Internet sales, the company recognizes that other large competitors will be selling tax-free over the Internet. Walmart does not want to be at a competitive disadvantage.

No Free Lunch

If state and local governments are aced out of an increasing proportion of potential sales taxes [from the Internet], they will simply have to raise other taxes—the property tax, payroll or income taxes—to make up the difference.

Tom Teepen, *Liberal Opinion*, December 27, 1999.

This approach by Walmart will be replicated by virtually every other company that is going on the Internet. The result will be a massive loss of the income state and local governments need to fund schools and other basic and needed services.

So, this is an important issue and one that needs a thoughtful response by Congress soon.

> "*Sales over the Internet are fast capturing the attention of tax-hungry politicians, but collecting sales taxes on Internet purchases poses logistical, as well as constitutional, problems.*"

The Government Should Not Tax Internet Commerce

Lawrence W. Reed

In the following viewpoint, Lawrence W. Reed argues that purchases made over the Internet should not be taxed. He contends that exempting Internet purchases from taxation is vital to continuing the expansion of local revenues that have resulted from the economic growth spurred by online commerce. In addition, tax-free Internet sales will not harm traditional stores, he maintains, because such stores will continue to enjoy an advantage over online businesses—customers can go into them and inspect products before they buy. Lawrence W. Reed is president of the Mackinac Center for Public Policy, a free-market research and education organization.

As you read, consider the following questions:

1. According to the author, by what percentage did state revenues grow between 1989 and 1995?
2. According to Reed, why does Adam Thierer believe that Internet taxes would result in "taxation without representation"?
3. By what percentage would Internet taxes reduce total spending on Internet transactions, according to Austan Goolsbee and Jonathan Zittrain?

Reprinted, with permission, from Lawrence W. Reed, "Don't Tax the Internet," *Ideas on Liberty*, June 2000.

On a visit to the Roman ruins at Volubulis, Morocco, I noticed a magnificent stone arch the city's officials erected nearly 2,000 years ago. Etched in stone and still eminently readable were Latin words thanking Emperor Caracalla for two things: protecting the city from invaders and exempting the citizens from taxation. Please excuse the ancient redundancy.

Leave the Web Alone

Caracalla was not generally known for his kindnesses. Indeed, he brutalized and persecuted many citizens of the Roman Empire. But that tax policy is the perfect answer to a burning question in America today: *Should states and localities tax the Internet?* What Caracalla did for Volubulis, our politicians ought to do for the Web. They should leave it alone. (Unfortunately, later Roman emperors *did* tax Volubulis and that's one reason why it's in ruins.)

Hungry Politicians and Chaos

Sales over the Internet are fast capturing the attention of tax-hungry politicians, but collecting sales taxes on Internet purchases poses logistical, as well as constitutional, problems. If 7,500 jurisdictions with sales taxes were to apply their own tax collection regimes to the Internet, America would experience tax pandemonium. To prevent chaos and allow for time to think about the issue, Congress in 1998 passed the Internet Tax Freedom Act, which instituted a national three-year moratorium on any taxes directed at electronic commerce.

State and local officials aren't upset because they're losing revenue. They're upset because they're missing out on a *new* source of revenue. South Dakota Governor William Janklow startled an audience when he declared that unless steps are taken to immediately tax online purchases, he may "disrupt interstate commerce" by sending out state highway patrol officers to pull over "little brown trucks," inspecting packages for those originating out of state, and then "following the packages" to their destination to force his residents to pay the state's sales tax.

The Internet taxation debate has produced tough questions that must be answered if this promising new sphere of enterprise is to grow unmolested by government. Here are a few of those questions, with some suggested answers.

Revenues and Traditional Sales

Has the growth of tax-free Internet sales hurt government revenues?

State governments are awash in tax revenues, with a total surplus in 2000 of $36 billion. *Investor's Business Daily* notes that state revenues grew 227 percent and local revenues grew 193 percent between 1980 and 1995.

Raymond J. Keating, chief economist for the Small Business Survival Committee, pointed out in testimony in 1999 that "federal, state and local governments have lost no revenues to expanding e-commerce, but have gained revenues due to economic growth driven in part by information technologies."

Instead of always worrying about whether government is getting enough of other people's money, we ought to be concerned about whether people are able to keep enough of what they earn to continue saving, investing, and baking a bigger economic pie for everyone.

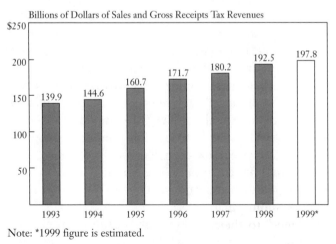

State and Local Sales Tax Revenues Continue to Rise Even as Internet Commerce Grows

Billions of Dollars of Sales and Gross Receipts Tax Revenues

Year	Value
1993	139.9
1994	144.6
1995	160.7
1996	171.7
1997	180.2
1998	192.5
1999*	197.8

Note: *1999 figure is estimated.

Source: Census Bureau, from http://www.census.gov/govs/www/qtax.html.

Is it "unfair" for sales over the Internet to be tax-free while more traditional sales are taxed?

No. In fact, it would be blatantly unfair to tax out-of-state vendors that do business in a state over the Internet. Taxes are supposed to pay for services that governments provide, such as police protection. As Adam Thierer of the Heritage Foundation has pointed out, "out-of-state vendors of electronic commerce, though subjected to the same tax burdens that Main Street vendors must bear, would receive none of the benefits for the taxes they paid to state and local governments where they did not reside. This amounts to a form of taxation without representation."

Web Should Continue to Grow

Would imposing new taxes on the Internet do serious damage to the ability of this new form of commerce to thrive?

A recent study by economists Austan Goolsbee of the University of Chicago and Jonathan Zittrain of Harvard University estimates that applying sales taxes to electronic commerce would reduce the number of online buyers by 25 percent and total spending on Internet transactions by more than 30 percent. The study suggests that these sales would not be replaced by ordinary retail sales, since the Internet is probably a net trade *creator*, generating business that would not otherwise have occurred.

Does the growth of online shopping pose a threat to traditional bricks-and-mortar retailers?

The most pertinent answer to that question is yet another question: Do catalog sales pose such a threat?

Like Internet sales, catalog sales involve greater convenience for the shopper. They've been a reality in America for decades. Yet catalog sales haven't devastated traditional retailers. Why? Because both catalog sales and e-commerce have—and always will have—a decisive disadvantage in relation to traditional retail sales: the inability of the consumer to examine the goods. And, of course, there's no need to charge for shipping.

The latest figures available bear out this counsel of common sense. E-commerce—while thriving—still only constitutes a tiny fraction—less than one percent—of all retail sales. E-commerce poses no danger of large income losses for traditional retailers. Indeed, the Web offers *new* sales opportunities for *every* business. Because setting up and maintaining a Web page is inexpensive, this is especially true for small firms.

Taxes Would Hurt the Poor

Does tax-free Internet shopping disproportionately hurt the poor?

No, quite the contrary. And applying taxes to the Internet would certainly not *help* the poor at all.

The pro-tax argument goes like this: Since low-income individuals are the least likely to have Internet access, they are the least able to shop online. The poor will end up paying the lion's share of sales taxes as wealthier citizens escape through untaxed Internet purchases.

A Trojan Horse Tax Scheme

The Internet tax debate is not about creating a level playing field between Main Street merchants and dot-com sellers. States already can tax—if they so choose—all catalog sales and Internet transactions. Instead, this debate is about whether politicians will use the Internet as a Trojan Horse for their true agenda: Creating a nation-wide sales-tax cartel to prevent taxpayers from being able to buy products where taxes are lower.

Daniel Mitchell, *Insight*, August 21, 2000.

"The Internet is especially valuable to inner-city residents," notes Aaron Lukas of the Cato Institute. "Lower-income urban shoppers can go online to find goods and services not available in their own neighborhoods, which often aren't served by traditional stores. A recent study conducted by PricewaterhouseCoopers and the Initiative for a Competitive Inner City concludes that "inner-city residents with access to computers and the Internet use the Web as often as, and sometimes more frequently than, does the general U.S. population."

Moreover, computer ownership and Internet access among low income people are growing at rates so rapid that some observers are predicting that every man, woman, and child in America will be connected to the Internet before [the year 2000].

The Internet represents a new world of enterprise, easily accessible to buyers and sellers alike. Rather than looking for ways to swipe some chunk of it, politicians should see it as a means to a better life for everyone.

> If "all artists offer their wares directly
> through the Web, I predict we will then
> discover that we have lost a crucial function
> we never gave record companies credit for:
> winnowing."

Music Distribution over the Internet Should Be Regulated

Randall E. Stross

Randall E. Stross argues in the following viewpoint that allow-ing unregulated exchange of free music over the Internet may destroy record companies and harm artists and consumers. He claims that record companies serve customers in a way that the Internet cannot duplicate: they cull out less-talented artists, which enables musicians with more potential—whom they subsidize—to succeed. Stross predicts that other industries dealing in intellectual property—such as book publishing—will likewise be destroyed if the sharing of their products over the Internet remains unregulated. Randall E. Stross writes for *U.S. News and World Report*.

As you read, consider the following questions:

1. According to Stross, who are the music industry's most prominent defenders?
2. Why is the author skeptical that websites like Napster will encourage consumers to purchase CDs?
3. What is the net profit that a record company realizes from the sale of one CD, according to Stross?

Microsoft's director of government relations. IVillage's chief financial officer. The Recording Industry Association of America's PR honcho. These professional explainers have some of the most unpleasant jobs I can think of at the moment.

The Napster Controversy

The music industry enjoys about as much sympathy from the public as does, oh, the tobacco industry. Its image is not helped by the recent Federal Trade Commission wrist slap for record companies' penalizing retailers that advertised deep discounts on CDs. Now, a string of unwelcome headlines have chronicled its legal war on Internet challengers, first MP3.com [a website that offers free music to download] and, more recently, Napster, the site that enables users to download songs that reside on the hard drives of other fans and are available free.

The music establishment's most prominent defenders, heavy-metal group Metallica and rapper Dr. Dre, have also attacked Napster, forcing it to close down the accounts of fans who have downloaded the performers' songs.

In retaliation, Napster supporters have made Metallica the butt of ridicule: Crowds of Web visitors have been enjoying a satiric, expletive-filled animated cartoon, "Napster Bad," starring two members of Metallica, developed by Campchaos.com. The cartoon drummer directs outrage at Napster users: "Just because you, like, made us rich, you think you can get free stuff, for stuff that we spend upwards of, you know, like, 24 to 48 hours writing and recording?" His sidekick is capable only of monosyllabic growls. His longest utterance: "Money good. Napster bad."

Some bands have come to Napster's defense. Limp Bizkit and Cypress Hill will make up part of the opposing tag team in this World Music Federation Smackdown. The two groups will go on a "Back to Basics" tour in 2000 flying the banner of Napster, which has put up $1.8 million to underwrite the free concerts.

Cut prices, get rich? The biggest surprise has come from *Wall Street Journal* technology columnist Walter Mossberg, who described Napster with uncharacteristic giddiness. So excited was Mossberg about his experience in the Napster "candy store" that he suggested that the music industry adopt an entirely new business model. Permit consumers to purchase and download a single song—for no more than 75 cents, he suggested helpfully—rather than force buyers to pay $16 for a CD with a dozen songs to obtain a single favorite track. Then Mossberg tried to argue that such deep price cuts would benefit the record companies because it would unleash untapped demand that would make up for the drop in per-unit revenue. His evidence? He personally bought five CDs after stumbling across artists found on Napster that he had forgotten about.

Would Artists Create for Free?

If I knew I wouldn't get paid much for writing a book because lots of people read it for free, I'm not sure I'd write it.

It turns out that if you don't protect intellectual property, most people won't bother creating things—not artists, not prescription-drug manufacturers, not writers and not musicians.

So here's my epiphany: Intellectual-property laws have given our country the edge in technology—and ironically, allowed us to have programs like [the free music sharing program] Napster. Without them, we wouldn't be the tech capital of the world. In the 16th century, for instance, the Spanish empire didn't protect ship designers, so they all moved to England, and then England turned around and kicked Spain's butt in some big, important war. England is still a big, important country. Have you ever even heard of Spain?

Joel Stein, *Time Digital*, 2000.

An expectation of resurgent CD sales flies in the face of common sense. Wasn't it Mossberg himself who lamented the 1:12 ratio of favorites to filler that one expects on the new CD purchased at the store? More likely, users will download their favorite songs free and "burn" their own compilation CDs: Twelve favorites out of every 12 tracks will always beat 1:12.

Napster's interim CEO, Eileen Richardson, is even more audacious in her claims: The record industry today is a $40 billion business, and Napster—by helping to make current titles available to one and all free—will build it into a $100 billion business. Why, of course!

Subsidizing the Not-Yet-Famous

If the industry is forced to adopt a pennies-per-song model, I'm not concerned about Metallica band members missing payments on their Ferraris. But I am concerned about what the implications are for the not-yet-famous bands that account for almost all of the 7,000 new CD titles that come out each year on the major labels—because the Metallicas and Dr. Dres subsidize the costs.

Consumers pick up a CD at the store and think the difference between the 60 cents it takes to make a disk and the $16 retail price is prima facie evidence of gouging. But the dreary economic facts are these: Subtract all the costs and the overhead that serves to support other artists under the same roof, and the net profit that the record company retains is about 59 cents per CD.

The same combination—low unit manufacturing costs and comparatively high retail price—is found in book publishing, and there, too, a few hits carry the entire list. Book publishers do not yet face the immediate threat that Napster and its successors pose for the music business. But the publishers know it is ahead, and there is plenty of hand-wringing about what can be done about it.

Free music, or almost free music, sounds sweet to me, too. But if record companies are destroyed by the "new economics," and all artists offer their wares directly through the Web, I predict we will then discover that we have lost a crucial function we never gave record companies credit for: winnowing. With the demise of business as usual, every garage band in existence will have equal standing in the undifferentiated mass of millions of titles thrown up on the Web. Yes, downloads will be inexpensive, but how will one find the good stuff? Then we'll belatedly realize that those demonized record companies once had saved us from ourselves.

> *"The U.S. Constitution allows Congress to enact copyright protections for authors 'to promote the progress of science and useful arts,' not to protect the special interests of Hollywood or music executives."*

Attempts to Regulate Music Distribution over the Internet Are Misguided

Phyllis Schlafly

In the following viewpoint, Phyllis Schlafly argues that sharing free music via websites like Napster is legal under fair-use applications of U.S. copyright law. She contends that the recording industry is working to make it illegal to share free music over the Internet simply to protect its domination of the music market. Schlafly predicts that websites like Napster will change the way people obtain music and other intellectual property, and that industries dealing in intellectual property will eventually profit from the expanded market. Phyllis Schlafly is a syndicated columnist.

As you read, consider the following questions:
1. According to Schlafly, what did the 1992 Audio Home Recording Act legalize?
2. What does the term "work for hire" mean, according to the author?
3. According to Schlafly, how did the advent of VCRs affect the move industry?

Reprinted from Phyllis Schlafly, "Future Meets Past in Napster Case," *Conservative Chronicle*, August 30, 2000, by permission of Copley News Service.

"This is a culture war, between the powers that were and that will be."

Is he talking about abortion? Gay rights? Hollywood violence? Illegitimacy? No, the culture war is about ownership and regulation of the Internet, according to John Perry Barlow, Grateful Dead lyricist and cyber rights activist.

Napster Versus the Music Cartel

Barlow may be right. The influence of the Internet may be overflowing into our culture, as well as our politics.

The current flash point of controversy about the Internet is a case in the Ninth Circuit Court of Appeals, *Recording Industry Association of American (RIAA) vs. Napster*, where the five giant music companies are fighting a web site called Napster for facilitating online music.[1] The music cartel wants to stop listening to music on the Internet.

Most music CDs are stamped with a warning that unauthorized duplication is prohibited by law, but this is not true. It's the same claim Hollywood made when trying to stop individuals from taping TV shows with VCRs, but the Supreme Court in 1984 ruled that unauthorized copying for the purpose of time-shifting is legitimate "fair use."

Furthermore, Congress specifically legalized the noncommercial consumer copying of digital music in the 1992 Audio Home Recording Act. The music cartel lobbied for this bill because its main purpose was to allow the cartel to control and impose a mandatory royalty on digital audio tape.

Artists Versus the Music Cartel

The political power of the music cartel in Washington, D.C., was also demonstrated in 1999 when it sneaked a law through Congress making music a "work for hire," i.e., the property of the recording companies rather than the musicians. Without any hearings or debate, this provision was buried in an unrelated bill as a "technical correction" and signed by President Bill Clinton.

Musicians were outraged that the law no longer considered them authors of their own music, and Sheryl Crow and

---

1. Verdict in the Napster case was still pending at press time.

other artists testified at a post-passage hearing of the House Intellectual Property subcommittee. Subcommittee Chairman Howard Coble, R-N.C., was unsympathetic, grumbling that he hoped rock star Don Henley (of Eagles fame) "gets carpal tunnel syndrome" from counting his money.

A Transformation in Music Distribution

Until very recently, almost all artists relied on record companies to provide the technology and business expertise needed to sell their work to the public. That began to change in 1987, when German engineers created a program that could compress computer sound files to about one-tenth of their normal size. Before that code was created, sound files took up too much storage space on computer discs, and were not practical for personal use. The compression method made it possible to convert music to files that were compact enough to store on personal computers and could be played back at near-CD quality. In 1992, the Moving Picture Experts Group (MPEG) of Italy used the compression method to create a format called MPEG 1-Audio Layer 3, or MP3.

Because they are compressed to take up a minimal amount of computer memory, MP3s and other types of music files, such as Liquid Audio, can be easily transmitted over the Internet. Some people trade MP3s via e-mail. One of the most popular ways to distribute and obtain music on-line is through "peer-to-peer" file-sharing programs such as Napster and Gnutella, which can be downloaded for free from the Internet.

Issues and Controversies on File, August 11, 2000.

The recording cartel backed down and agreed to the repeal of this law. The music cartel usually gets what it wants: In recent years it has gotten Congress to pass a copyright term extension, draconian criminal penalties on small incidents of copyright infringement and a law to criminalize "circumvention" of the wishes of a copyright owner.

Copyright Law

For years, the music cartel was coercing retailers to sell CDs at the manufacturer's suggested retail price, a violation of antitrust law. The Federal Trade Commission (FTC) stopped this price-fixing scheme and 28 states are now suing for hundreds of millions of dollars in damages.

The music cartel desperately wants to shut down Napster and similar web sites that facilitate the non-commercial sharing of music. The big five labels are frightened that on-line music may upset their out-of-date business practices.

The U.S. Constitution allows Congress to enact copyright protections for authors "to promote the progress of science and useful arts," not to protect the special interests of Hollywood or music executives. Copyright holders have certain temporary rights but, under fair-use applications, so do consumers, and that's what the music cartel and other powerful interests are trying to eliminate through Internet regulation.

The Internet is a medium for peer-to-peer communication. The phone company doesn't regulate who we call or what we say on the phone, and the music industry should not be regulating Internet connections.

Nor should anyone be regulating information on how to use products in a manner that has been traditionally and legally considered fair use. Unfortunately, the Digital Millennium Copyright Act [which became law in 1998] was intended, by Hollywood and others who lobbied for it, to give copyright owners a measure of control they never had before.

A 16-year-old Norwegian kid figured out a code that allows people to view legitimately purchased DVD movies on Linux computers, even though Hollywood rigged these movies to be playable only on Windows computers and other machines. Now, Hollywood is suing everyone who spreads the word about the DVD code, including a magazine called *2600* and one guy who put the code on a T-shirt.

Changing Distribution Models

Despite scare stories, new technologies have nearly always expanded markets and created new opportunities for profits. Hollywood fought VCRs in Congress and all the way to the Supreme Court, and lost every battle in spite of doom-and-gloom predictions about how VCRs would ruin the industry.

It turned out that videotaped movies became a financial bonanza for Hollywood. We can also tape music over radio, but radio did not ruin the music market.

I have shelves of CDs I never listen to, but I'd buy a lot more if I could conveniently and easily find the music I really like. But the music cartel has blocked the online sale of the music it controls, and sites such as emusic.com have only fringe music.

Even though new technologies tend to disrupt current business models, legislative or judicial attempts to protect economically inefficient distribution channels are misguided.

Periodical Bibliography

The following articles have been selected to supplement the diverse views presented in this chapter. Addresses are provided for periodicals not indexed in the *Readers' Guide to Periodical Literature*, the *Alternative Press Index*, the *Social Sciences Index*, or the *Index to Legal Periodicals and Books*.

David Banisar	"Big Browser Is Watching You," *Index on Censorship*, March 2000.
John Perry Barlow	"A Declaration of the Independence of Cyberspace," *Humanist*, May/June 1996.
Dennis K. Berman	"Why Napster Is Good News," *Business Week*, August 7, 2000.
Robert Coles	"Safety Lessons for the Internet," *New York Times*, October 11, 1997.
Joseph L. Dionne	"Making Room for Privacy in the Global Village," *Christian Science Monitor*, August 5, 1997.
Michael S. Greve	"Yes, Tax the 'Net," *Weekly Standard*, May 15, 2000. Available from 1211 Avenue of the Americas, New York, NY 10036.
Stephen Levy	"On the Net, Anything Goes," *Newsweek*, July 7, 1997.
Greg Miller	"Consumer Privacy May Be More Secure Online than Off," *Los Angeles Times*, May 13, 1999. Available from Times Mirror Square, Los Angeles, CA 90053.
Daniel Mitchell	"Plan to Tax Internet Sales Would Turn the Constitution Upside Down," *Insight*, August 21, 2000. Available from 3600 New York Ave. NE, Washington, DC 20002.
Alexandra Samuel and Abby Scher	"Cookies Are Not So Sweet," *Dollars and Sense*, January/February 2000.
Nicholas Thompson	"Harlot's Web," *Washington Monthly*, November 1999.
Lars Ulrich	"It's Our Property," *Newsweek*, June 5, 2000.

CHAPTER 4

What Will Be the Future of the Internet?

Chapter Preface

The Internet in its embryonic stage appeared in 1969 as a communications network used primarily by academic researchers and scientists. As the medium became increasingly commercialized in the 1990s, however, thousands of consumers began to log on, which slowed down the speed of data transmission. Academics—frustrated by the traffic jams and speed limits of the commercial Internet—decided to create a network that they would not have to share with consumers. The fruit of their labors was Internet2, a collaboration among U.S. research universities, the National Science Foundation, and several technology companies.

Internet2 uses an existing high-speed national network that has been used for years to connect federal supercomputer centers. Most universities receive grants from the National Science Foundation to pay for the cost of connecting to the network. Once connected, academics from participating schools can share large data files such as complex computer models of the human ear that allow users to embark on "virtual" tours of the ear's inner structures. Internet2 also allows the transmission of real-time sound recordings, such as Chopin's *Polonaise in A-flat Minor.*

Although Internet2 was created as an alternative to the commercial Internet, many analysts predict that the hardware and software being developed to serve the academic community will one day be utilized on the public Internet. As *Washington Post* staff writer Rajiv Chandrasekaran reports, "the [Internet2] software and hardware would be purchased by commercial Internet service providers, resulting in faster access for average users." Ironically, as the academic community tries to re-establish an exclusive network such as they enjoyed before commercial interests bogged down the Internet, their innovations will likely improve the speed of the commercial Internet that they abandoned, possibly making Internet2 obsolete. The authors in the following chapter discuss other innovations and developments that will shape the future of the Internet. Most likely, the Internet will continue to be directed by strong academic and commercial interests, just as it has been in the past.

> *"Let's face it: this technology is for the
> world's information elite—those well off
> enough to afford the hardware and the
> local service provider's fees."*

The Internet Will Serve the World's Elite

Kunda Dixit

Kunda Dixit contends in the following viewpoint that for the most part the Internet will intensify social inequities because only those who can afford to buy computers and pay for Internet service—usually people from Western countries—will be able to use it. In consequence, he maintains that the Internet will spread Western culture and languages at the expense of non-Western societies, which will destroy cultural diversity worldwide. Dixit also argues that the Internet exacerbates global environmental problems such as the loss of biodiversity because it encourages the consumption of the Earth's finite resources. Kunda Dixit is a journalist from Nepal.

As you read, consider the following questions:
1. According to Dixit, what is the "Silicon Plateau"?
2. What is "cultural evaporation," according to Wolfgang Sachs?
3. According to the author, how will the Internet affect the world's languages?

Reprinted, with permission, from Kunda Dixit, "The Third Wave and the Third World," *Choices*, July 1997.

The official state visit to India by Microsoft president Bill Gates in March 1997 had all the glitter of a potentate touring a far-flung outpost of his global cyber-empire. In the media, Gates got the kind of red-carpet treatment usually reserved for victorious cricketers, or fellow billionaires like Michael Jackson. He managed to meet the prime minister twice and talked expansively about information technology as the tool that would finally lift India out of poverty. Gates went on to Johannesburg and suggested the same about Africa.

Cyber-Panacea

Cyber-panacea seems to be the credo in the virtual-reality universe of computer gurus. But it is going to take more than the polite remarks of a visiting business magnate for India to make the technological leap from the potato chip to the microchip. In an age of economic globalization, thousands of computer nerds slaving away in the software sweatshops of Bangalore's "Silicon Plateau" are probably helping Microsoft shareholders more than they are helping India.

Given all the hype, it is tempting for countries like India and others in the South to believe that information technology is the cure-all that will suddenly set things right. Development did not work, structural adjustment failed, free trade hasn't helped the really poor, so let's try the Internet. The World Wide Web of criss-crossing data will level the playing field, democratize information and benefit all, say some observers. But if history has taught us anything it is this: technology by itself is never the answer.

In Bangkok, I can now log onto the local website of a multinational pizza conglomerate, and a double-cheese pepperoni is at my doorstep in half an hour. The information revolution has become a lazy way to do home-shopping and a cheap and instantaneous postal system for my niece to request music videos from Asia's favourite video jockey in Hong Kong. Billions of gigabytes of information whiz around the world in nanoseconds. This information can be linked, making it possible to regard individual computer hosts as neurons and the wired planet as one large brain. But biologically, human beings have not evolved so fast: the speed, volume and intricacy of information has exceeded human capacity to grasp it all.

For the Information Elite

All this "cyberbole" has the danger of distracting us from what really matters. What is it that we are communicating? Does it have any use? Does it add up to knowledge? Obsessed with the quantity and speed of its transmission, we seem to have lost track of information *quality*.

In the media, technological advances have tended to make information even more events-oriented and one-sided. New digital encyclopedias and websites only mean a change of medium, not of content. Instead of Eurocentric history books, we now have Eurocentric multi-media disks in which you can actually see and hear Winston Churchill's famous speeches. A CD-ROM cinema archive I recently bought in Singapore includes only videos of Hollywood oldies: there is scant reference to renowned European directors, and even fewer mentions of Japanese, Indian or African ones.

Let's face it: this technology is for the world's information elite—those well off enough to afford the hardware and the local service provider's fees. And whatever the apostles of Bill Gates may say about the brave new world of information liberation, for the moment it is still very much a case of garbage-in-garbage-out. It may be just as well that the poor can't afford to log on.

The fact that computer ads have started resembling automobile commercials provides further proof that information technology is targeted for the privileged few. There is the same obsession with design, speed and the call for a spirit of adventure. The planned obsolescence of cars has its parallel in the never-ending cycle of annual software and hardware upgrades, which in the end just widen the gap between the "knows and the know-nots." Added all up, the corporate values that drive information technology are the same ones that messed up the earth. And industry's techno-fundamentalism diverts attention from the urgent political and economic measures needed to avert irreversible human-induced damage to the ecosphere, the loss of cultural and biological diversity, and the social inequities brought about by globalization.

Cultural Evaporation

Now, mix information technology with a worldwide free market and you have today's great globalizer. International media carry with them monocultural messages that result in what German ecologist Wolfgang Sachs calls "cultural evaporation": the erosion of diversity and its replacement by a uniform value system. There are still more than 5,000 languages spoken throughout the world, and only one per cent of them are of European origin. But as with biodiversity, variations on the spoken word are also dying out: at present rates, the whole world will speak only a few languages (mainly European) by the middle of the twenty-first century. The Internet's linguistic imperialism could speed up the process.

Internet Optimism Is Just Egocentric Ramblings

Not everyone can afford the cost of living in cyberspace.

Not only does operating a computer and keeping up with the latest technology demand a direct expense. Some people have other things to do with their time, such as working in non-technical occupations in order to feed, clothe, and house themselves. And many people are unable to even fulfill these basic needs. Thus, the uncritical optimism about the future is little more than egocentric ramblings of predominantly middle/upper class North Americans and West Europeans.

John Horvath, *Toward Freedom*, September/October 1997.

And while we may think we live in the age of information, more and more of it is completely useless in working out answers to global problems or defining lifestyles suited to a planet with finite resources. Instead of helping us find solutions, global television and its corporate ownership propagate reckless consumerism as a model for the rest of the world. And as they battle for higher ratings by stooping to the lowest common denominator in audience surveys, multimedia empires become the chief conduits for mainstream global values.

News is what editors in Atlanta or London decide the world should know. They mix their factoids with escapist amusement and beam it to all corners of the earth. Even if channel-surfing viewers can find a news bulletin amid all the background radiation of talk shows, mini-series and sports—and then stay tuned in long enough to inform themselves about what is really going on—the news itself comes across as increasingly surreal. In a Himalayan hamlet, six days' walk from the nearest road, I once watched the live TV murder trial of American football player O.J. Simpson, after the latest episode of "LA Law."

Television's convergence with computers and telecommunications is already revolutionizing the nature, speed and accessibility of information. If this aggravates the present information overload, it will bury what is essential even deeper under an avalanche of shallow words and superficial images.

A Runaway Juggernaut

The consensus seems to be: if you can't beat 'em, join 'em. Information technology is a runaway juggernaut, and it is better to ride it than get trampled. So, deep in the rainforests of southern Mexico, the Zapatista guerrilla leader subcommandante Marcos gives interviews via the Internet. The New People's Army in the Philippines, now with its own website, wages protracted guerrilla war against the military in the thickets of cyberspace.

Across the world, non-governmental organizations (NGOs), human rights activists, national liberation movements, indigenous groups from the Ogoni to the Karens have found silicon bonding in the horizontal communication provided by the Internet. Its inherent anarchy, decentralized nature and freedom from official control have made it the ideal medium. Alternative media are flourishing because of the low cost of electronic delivery, making it possible to bypass national controls. There is talk of using the new technology to leapfrog development by bringing decision-making and distance education to the grassroots.

But the verdict is still out on the potential benefits of information technology: epic battles between techno-fundamentalists [who embrace technology] and neo-Luddites [who are suspicious of technology] have bogged down every seminar or workshop on the subject that I have attended in the past year. Mimicking the computer's binary code, we tend to argue about information technology in terms of either/or, good/evil, centralizing/decentralizing, globalizing/localizing.

The future of information technology is probably going to be an analog mishmash of it all. There are parts of the world that are going to be colonized; others will break free riding the crest of a cyberwave. Indigenous languages may disappear on Irian Jaya, but Bahasa Indonesia with its Latin script could curb the inroad of English. Some countries may try to control information, but an unprecedented diversity of alternative viewpoints will always be available in newsgroups. Multinationals will cash in on the commercial potential of the Web, but savvy producers from the South will also be able to reach buyers for organically-grown tea or to market jute bags through sites like The Earth Market Place. Radio may still be in the hands of the state, but it may soon be possible to listen to audio files on sites like OneWorld Online.

The degree to which people can benefit from the Internet's potential for democratization, bring about true decentralization, or spread knowledge and education will depend on how much support the information-poor get to log on. At present, only donor-funded NGOs and research centres in the South can afford to buy computers, get phones and connect them to the Net; it is still a luxury for state-run universities, teachers and students. And what about telecommunications? Fewer than one in ten people in India has a telephone. The limiting factor is not that Indians cannot afford computers and modems; it is the high price and lack of phone lines.

Maybe Bill Gates should invest in telephones first.

> *"The Internet is providing the means for ordinary citizens to subvert long-existing power structures."*

Individuals Will Become Empowered by the Internet

Matthew R. Estabrook

In the following viewpoint, Matthew R. Estabrook argues that the Internet empowers individuals because it increases their access to information. He contends that the Internet has increased competition among traditional power structures—such as governments and media conglomerates—which has given ordinary citizens more choice. Indeed, Estabrook predicts that such a shifting of power may result in governments that are more responsive to citizens' needs. Matthew R. Estabrook is manager for Education and Training at the Center for Market Processes in Fairfax, Virginia.

As you read, consider the following questions:
1. What effect did Gutenberg's printing press have on the Protestant Reformation, according to the author?
2. According to Estabrook, by what percentage has the number of people accessing the Internet been increasing each month?
3. How did the Internet help people after the Kobe earthquake, according to the author?

Reprinted, with permission, from Matthew R. Estabrook, "Internet Revolution Can Empower People," *Human Events*, February 16, 1996.

J ohann Gutenberg's invention of movable type printing enabled ideas to be circulated widely and cheaply for the first time. This free flow of ideas was a critical catalyst for the Protestant Reformation. In the 1980s the desktop computer and fax machine played an important role in the process that led to the breakup of the Soviet Union.

The Digital Printing Press

Today, thanks to the Internet, technology may be bringing on another information revolution. In 1995, *Time* magazine reported that some Iranian scholars have gained access to the Internet, exposing them for the first time to the ideas of Shakespeare, Mill, and other Westerners. Iran's government may find it increasingly difficult to contain this information flow.

Today, what we call the Internet is a vast "mega-network" of 50,000 computer networks in 90 different countries. Thirty million people access the Internet through telephone lines and personal computers, send electronic mail, download computer software, buy products, and gather news and information. The number has been increasing about 10% each month.

The Internet provides not only access to information and ideas, but the power to distribute them as well. Gutenberg's printing press reduced the costs of sharing information a thousandfold. Innovations such as the photocopier and more desktop publishing have further reduced these costs, enabling even individuals to produce professional documents inexpensively.

The Internet takes this information revolution even further; now, one doesn't even need paper to publish his ideas widely. Empowering people in this way has reduced the influence of the traditional media.

For years, information on world affairs came from a limited array of sources: the Big Three networks, a few national radio syndicates, and several large newspapers and news services. That has begun to change. Cable brought with it CNN and C-SPAN, and a host of other stations that cater to the varied tastes and needs of segments of the population. Talk radio has emerged as a new forum through which people can

166

express their views. And now the Internet, with its host of real-time chat conversations, E-mail lists, and news groups, offers new ways for people to share information.

Common Interests, Goals, and Values

The Internet also allows each individual to choose his own community. Typically, when we think of community, we think of the people who live in our apartment building or neighborhood, but the Internet allows us to converse with whomever we please.

Technology makes it almost as easy to communicate with someone in Japan as with someone around the block. The Internet has therefore fostered the growth of new, virtual communities that are not bound by arbitrary physical borders, but by common interests, goals, and values.

A Seat at the Table of Democracy

The fact that so many people are now connected, via the Internet, with far more to connect in the future, has given rise to the idea of online democracy, where people are actually able to vote through their computer. That's crucial in more ways than one, because along with ideas, and the ability to shape them, comes the accessibility to those ideas by people who may have felt excluded in the past. People with disabilities who may find it difficult to have their ideas heard in a traditional setting, elderly people who find travel difficult, or simply people whose lives or income level make it difficult to attend face-to-face meetings or public forums are now enabled to take a seat at the discussion table through online forums.

Andrew Hammer, *Democratic Left*, 1999.

For example, the Internet proved the only effective channel of communication between survivors of the 1995 Kobe earthquake in Japan and their friends and families around the world. In the United States, several pages emerged on the World Wide Web hours after the 1995 Oklahoma City bombing, documenting the destruction and offering help and support to those in need.

Perhaps most important, the Internet is providing the means for ordinary citizens to subvert long-existing power structures, especially the taxes, tariffs, and regulations imposed by governments. As businesses rely increasingly on human capital (knowledge and information) and less on physical capital, tariffs become increasingly irrelevant.

Likewise, entrepreneurs may establish banks and investment firms wherever the tax and regulatory burdens are least oppressive, and continue to serve customers anywhere in the world. At least one enterprise offers Internet users the opportunity to gamble legally on sporting events. Based offshore, it is not subject to the laws which forbid such operations in most of the United States.

Lofty purposes? Not always, but the Internet, by facilitating the spread of information, is restoring power to individuals to make choices that affect their own lives and is undermining outside interference in the process.

How will governments respond to this rapid decentralization of knowledge and power? Perhaps they will be forced to compete with one another to create friendlier environments for trade. The result could be governments with simpler, less burdensome regulations and taxes.

This may not be far-fetched. After all, government regulation is likely to run at least a step behind an adaptive order that taps the knowledge of all its participants. That would be another information-based revolution.

| *"We will be able to link every individual*
| *and every machine via cyberspace."*

The Internet Will Spark a Communications Revolution

Jennifer L. Schenker

In the following viewpoint, Jennifer L. Schenker reports that the Internet will revolutionize communications by linking people in remote locations with machines that can assist them, allowing people to connect over the Internet in real time, and giving users a multisensory online experience. She explains that Internet speed and reliability will increase in order to accommodate this increase in online services. In addition, Schenker notes that users will enjoy more protection of their personal information as privacy-guarding technologies improve. Jennifer L. Schenker writes for *Time* magazine.

As you read, consider the following questions:
1. According to Schenker, what is "Embed the Internet"?
2. What are "buddy systems," according to the author?
3. According to the author, what is "digitalme"?

You are driving down the autobahn near Stuttgart and something goes wrong with the engine of your car. Before you even realize there is a problem, the car has sent an e-mail detailing the trouble to the automaker's portal site on the Internet. The website figures out where the closest dealer is and sends a message there, and employees check the stockroom for the necessary parts and pencil in the next available slot with a mechanic. By the time an e-mail arrives at your dashboard computer alerting you to the fault, you are presented with the solution as well.

This scenario, envisioned by Hewlett Packard, is what Peter van der Fluit, Hewlett Packard Europe's vice president and general manager of enterprise marketing, calls "chapter two of the Internet. We will be able to link every individual and every machine via cyberspace." In addition to owners of personal computers, anyone with a car, mobile phone, personal digital assistant (P.D.A.) or TV will be connected to the Internet. Not to mention those wearing tennis shoes. In future, microchips in running shoes will monitor the body's vital signs. "In 20 years' time it will be odd for something not to be on the network," says Bill Joy, chief scientist and corporate executive officer at Sun Microsystems.

Between now and 2005, personalized "follow-me-everywhere" services will become commonplace; business and economy-class Web services will be introduced; and consumers will take control of their digital identities. Not only will the Net support a variety of new access devices, but it will become the primary vehicle for voice, data and video transmission. Already, a group of communication giants, including AT&T, has formed an alliance called Embed the Internet, which aims to accelerate the market for globally networked, intelligent devices in homes, offices and factories worldwide. And we'll see the introduction of pocket-sized devices that "know what you want, where you are and what is next," predicts Joy.

Putting everything and everyone on the Net will open up new commercial opportunities. For example, when you visit a new place your mobile device—knowing your preferences— will automatically suggest the restaurants that serve your favorite wines and foods, list the shows you might like to see, then provide you with maps of how to get there, says Joy, whose company Sun is developing Jini, a networking system to automatically link computing devices. Or, say your car breaks down before you get to the dealer. While you are stuck on the highway, a cyberspace services broker—accessible from a range of portable devices—would in minutes be able to electronically arrange for a tow truck to pick you up and order a rental car to be waiting at the dealership. That's the idea behind Hewlett Packard's new E-services, launched in May [1999], which electronically link up buyers and sellers who have had no prior contact and may want to do business with each other only once.

Overall, it is going to become much easier for people to communicate over the Net. "Buddy systems"—which alert people when their friends and relatives are on the Net and ready to chat—are just the beginning. Communicating with others in real time—rather than waiting for an e-mailed reply—will soon be the norm. Real-time multilingual communications mean that people will be able to ask a question of a company's customer service department, for example, in whatever language they feel most comfortable, and the message will be routed to the most knowledgeable person in the firm regardless of where they are and what language they speak. Although the answer might be given in Cantonese, the questioner will instantly receive the answer in their own language, thanks to instant messaging and "on the fly" language translation. These technologies create a kind of real-time, multilingual intercom, says John Patrick, vice president of Internet technology at IBM. IBM plans to offer this capability in its WebSphere Application Server software and its Lotus division's Sametime E-meetings technology.

Business-to-business electronic commerce will also become easier thanks to a new technical standard called XML (extensible markup language) that makes it simpler to interconnect different kinds of business computing systems, thus allowing suppliers, manufacturers and distributors to more easily exchange orders and information. Access to the best medical advice, education courses and museums is also set to improve. Kenan Sahin, vice president of software technology at Bell Labs and president of Lucent's Kenan Systems subsidiary, says the Internet will increasingly become a multisensory experience. "The Internet will allow people to experience art in the real sense of the word by feeling the texture and smelling the aroma," he says. "Imagine using the Internet to walk through a museum in Paris, then to sit online in a sidewalk cafe to discuss your visit with a Parisian. You communicate through interfaces so realistic that you see the excitement in his eyes, hear the subtlest nuance in his voice and smell the coffee he's drinking."

Realistic interfaces will also add a much more human element to online business meetings, gatherings of friends or shopping transactions. With optical recognition software, a businesswoman could have her personal video camera identify as a competitor or a prospect a person entering a crowded room. And shoppers could inspect merchandise thanks to a "hands-free" computer interface that uses small television cameras to register the position of a person's hands in front of a computer screen. The person moves her hands to control the computer and grasp or turn images of objects projected onto a three-dimensional screen.

Teleworld

When you walk into a room in your teleworld [linked to the Internet] home, you will be detected and tracked like a FedEx parcel. Your presence will trigger the room to adapt to your environmental preferences; it will tell musical playback units to turn on your favorite selections and adjust the room temperature to your comfort zone. In short, the physical environment will adjust to your requirements and preferences.

Raymond K. Neff, *World & I*, May 2000.

All of these applications will take bandwidth [the width of the conduit that transmits data over a network]—and lots of it. Some of the sector's biggest companies are working on making the Internet 1,000 times faster and more reliable. But once everything from supercomputers to toasters is online, won't that result in the mother of all traffic jams on the information superhighway? DiffServ is designed to prevent that. Under the plan, the Internet will be split into a six-lane highway with slow lanes, normal lanes and passing lanes.

Each data packet will carry a little electronic flag identifying its lane. Internet service providers will charge accordingly, just as travelers pay different fares for first or second class. "All data packets are not equal," says IBM's Patrick. "Some should get priority over others."

The system is supposed to give consumers flexibility, allowing them to reserve bandwidth when they need it. This would enable a traveling businesswoman, for example, to engage in a video conference with a client from wherever she happens to be. This kind of consumer would be happy to pay a premium for guaranteed bandwidth and quality of service. But some consumers won't mind slower service under certain circumstances, and some businesses will take advantage of the lower tariffs for lower speeds to create new services.

Ken Blakeslee, vice president of business development for Carrier and Wireless Solutions at Nortel Networks, uses the example of a teenage boy out rollerblading with his friends. The Web-enabled Gameboy on his wrist beeps to notify him that the latest version of his favorite game has just come out. Would he like to download it for $4.95? Since he already has a payment account, all he has to do is push the O.K. button. During the next two hours, as he skates around the park with his friends, the video game will be downloaded.

Or say a businessman wants to buy a new home in a distant city. He uses the phone built into his spectacles to call a real-estate agent. The agent selects virtual tours of available homes and sends them to the businessman's wearable computer at a slow bit rate. Happy to walk through the interactive tours that evening after the images are downloaded, the businessman will also have the option of sampling the images at any time by using the visual receivers built into the lenses of his glasses. "Any information you don't need immediately is a candidate for lower-speed, lower-priced transmission," says Lucent's Sahin. Blakeslee compares it to the strategy of airlines, which often sell the same seats for vastly different prices. For airlines the goal is to fill the plane; for Internet service providers, it is to fill the network.

While technology enthusiasts tout the advantages of all these new services, others point to a darker side—loss of privacy. Managing digital identity is a critical issue for both consumers and businesses and is a major source of friction between the U.S. government and the European Commission. Consumers are looking to wrest away from Internet companies control over the electronic collection of personal information such as bookmarks and credit card details. Now, new products are hitting the market that allow consumers to control exactly how much information they give out. For example, NCR Corp., which makes software used by financial organizations and retailers to compile information about consumers, has come out with a product that permits consumers to opt into or out of personal data collection. Novell's "digitalme," expected to be available in January [2000], uses a business card metaphor to manage identity. The same "mecard" might give out your home address and phone plus mobile number to friends, but only flash an e-mail address to a corporation. The digitalme system can be programmed to fill in the forms used to register and establish access privileges on many websites. It then monitors what the websites do with your personal information and creates a log of where your details have been forwarded. Earlier this year [1999], IBM and partner Equifax launched digital certificate products and services that help consumers identify the people and organizations with whom they do online business. A digital certificate can be used to establish a person's online identity and define their relationships within a certain business or group, much like a passport or driver's license. Digital certificates also allow users to encrypt and send information over networks without the fear that unauthorized persons can open the data.

IBM's Patrick says that with these new safeguards, putting personal information online is something consumers should embrace, not fear. "Look at your medical records and think of where they are today," he says. "Most likely they are in manila folders in multiple doctors' offices with no controls over who reads them." The best solution to this problem, he says, is to go digital. If Patrick is right, then a lot more than just book purchases and credit card details will be going online in the not-too-distant future.

> *"The Internet as a technology . . . will not free us from a world where Wall Street and Madison Avenue have control over our journalism and culture."*

Media Conglomerates Will Control the Internet

Robert McChesney

Robert McChesney argues in the following viewpoint that media giants such as Disney and Time Warner will control content on the Internet. He contends that with their economic power and domination of the traditional media market, these corporations have squeezed out all competitors and have commercialized the Internet. McChesney asserts that the only way to democratize the Internet is for more nonprofit and small commercial entities to establish an online presence. Robert McChesney is a research associate professor at the University of Illinois and author of the book *Rich Media, Poor Democracy: Communication Politics in Dubious Times*, from which this viewpoint was adapted.

As you read, consider the following questions:
1. According to McChesney, how much less do households with access to the Internet watch television than those in unwired homes?
2. What portion of the thirty-one most-visited news and entertainment websites were affiliated with large media firms in 1998, according to McChesney?
3. How much did online advertising amount to in 1997, according to the author?

Reprinted, with permission, from Robert McChesney, "The Titanic Sails On," *Extra!* March/April 2000.

The January 2000 announcement of the proposed merger of America Online (AOL) and Time Warner—the largest deal in history—crystallizes one trend, and may trigger another, more ominous one.

Media Mergers

It can be seen as yet another of the colossal media deals that have dotted the past decade, such that only a handful of conglomerates now own almost all the film studios, TV networks, music studios, cable TV channels and much, much, more. But more than that, the deal represents what may be the first great move toward convergence, where the handful of giants who dominate computer software, the Internet and media begin to formally merge with each other.

This all makes sense, because as everything switches to digital language, the technical distinctions between these categories recede and are ultimately nonexistent. The end result of this process—five, 10 or 15 years down the line—may be an integrated global communication market dominated by no more than a dozen (often closely linked) firms of unfathomable size and economic and political power. By any known standard of a free press in a democratic society, these developments should provoke intense concern, if not outrage.

False Prophesies

In the wake of the AOL/Time Warner announcement, their executives and defenders pooh-poohed the idea that, in the Age of the Internet, we have any grounds for concern that our media and communication systems are in too few hands. The Internet, we are told, has blasted open the communication system and increased exponentially the ability of consumers to choose from the widest imaginable array of choices. If everything is in the process of becoming digital, if anyone can produce a website at minimal cost, and if it can be accessed worldwide via the World Wide Web, it is only a matter of time (e.g., expansion of bandwidth, improvement of software) before the media giants find themselves swamped by countless high-quality competitors. Their monopolies will be crushed.

The Electronic Frontier Foundation's John Perry Barlow, in a memorable comment from 1995, dismissed concerns about media mergers and concentration. The big media firms, Barlow noted, are "merely rearranging deck chairs on the Titanic." The "iceberg," he submitted, would be the Internet with its 500 million channels.

Clearly, the Internet is changing the nature of our media landscape radically. As Barry Diller, builder of the Fox TV network and a legendary corporate media seer, put it, "We're at the very early stages of the most radical transformation of everything we hear, see, know."

But will these changes pave the way for a qualitatively different and better media culture and society? Or will the corporate, commercial system merely don a new set of clothing? The evidence so far strongly suggests that, left to the market, the Internet is going in a very different direction from that suggested by the Internet utopians. The Internet as a technology, in short, will not free us from a world where Wall Street and Madison Avenue have control over our journalism and culture.

Big Media Go Online

The main argument made by defenders of the AOL/Time Warner deal, and by defenders of the media status quo, is that the Internet is going to launch innumerable new commercially viable competitors, such that any concerns about concentrated corporate control are unfounded. If anything, the AOL/Time Warner deal should have hammered the last nail in the coffin of that argument. It is now clear that the Internet will probably not spawn any new commercially viable media entities; the media giants will rule the roost. Indeed, the Internet is encouraging even greater media concentration, not to mention convergence.

This might seem a bizarre assertion, since the big media firms have seemed to approach the Internet in such a bewildered and clumsy manner. Time Warner's Pathfinder website, for example, began in 1994 with visions of conquering the Internet, only to produce a "black hole" for the firm's balance sheet. Likewise, the New Century Network, a website consisting of 140 newspapers run by nine of the largest newspaper chains, was such a fiasco that it was shut down in 1998.

Far from being visionary, the initial motivation for media firms to dominate the Internet is as much fear as it is the prospects of mega-profits. "For traditional media companies," the *New York Times* correctly noted, "the digital age poses genuine danger." "The entertainment companies are terrified of being blindsided by the Internet," a business consultant said in the *Economist*, "as the broadcasting networks were blindsided by cable in the 1980s."

Titan in the Making

If America Online and Time Warner complete their merger, they would create the world's biggest media company.

Company	World Revenue (billion)
AOL/Time Warner	$41.0 billion
Disney	24.8
Vivendi/Seagram*	16.6
Viacom	14.8
Bertelsmann	14.8
News Corp.	14.1
Sony†	10.8

World Revenue
Four quarters
ended June 2000

*Media portions of Vivendi Seagram combined; total is $76.1 billion
†The media portions of Sony; total is $60.4 billion

New York Times, November 13, 2000.

In fact, it remains unclear exactly how the Internet will become a commercially viable media content enterprise. It is clear that there is a huge market for Internet Service Providers (e.g., AOL) and for electronic commerce (e.g., Amazon.com), but profits for online ventures that operate more like traditional media outlets are less assured. As Time Warner CEO Gerald Levin put it, it is "not clear where you make money on it." But even if the Internet takes a long time to develop as a commercial medium, it is already taking up some of the time that people used to devote to traditional media. An AC Nielsen study conducted late in 1998 determined that Internet homes watched 15 percent less television overall than unwired homes.

Mission Critical

Since 1998, all major media have made the Internet "mission critical," as Disney CEO Michael Eisner put it, and have launched significant web activities. The media firms use their websites, at the very least, to stimulate interest in their traditional fare—a relatively inexpensive way to expand sales. Some media firms duplicate their traditional publications or even broadcast their radio and television signals over the net (with commercials included, of course). The newspaper industry has rebounded from the New Century Network debacle, and has a number of sites to capture classified advertising dollars as they go online.

But most media giants are going beyond this on the Web. Viacom has extensive websites for its CBS Sports, MTV and Nickelodeon cable TV channels, the point of which is to produce "online synergies." These synergies can be produced by providing an interactive component and additional editorial dimensions to what is found in the traditional fare, but the main way websites produce synergies is by offering electronic commerce options for products related to the site. Several other commercial websites have incorporated Internet shopping directly into their editorial fare. As one media executive notes in *Advertising Age*, Web publishers "have to think like merchandisers." Electronic commerce is now seen as a significant revenue stream for media websites.

In conjunction with this upsurge in media giant Internet activity, the possibility of new Internet content providers emerging to slay the traditional media appears farfetched. In 1998 there was a massive shakeout in the online media industry, as smaller players could not remain afloat. Forrester Research estimated that the cost of an "average-content" website increased threefold to $3.1 million by 1998, and would double again by 2000. "While the big names are establishing themselves on the Internet," *The Economist* wrote, "the content sites that have grown organically out of the new medium are suffering." Even a firm with the resources of Microsoft flopped in its attempt to become an online content provider, abolishing much of its operation in 1998. "It's a fair comment to say that entertainment on the Internet did not pan out as expected," said a Microsoft executive.

By 1998, the current pattern was established: more than three-quarters of the 31 most-visited news and entertainment websites were affiliated with large media firms, and most of the rest were connected to outfits like AOL and Microsoft.

Why the Iceberg Didn't Hit

We can see now that those who forecast that the media giants would smash into the Internet "iceberg" exaggerated the power of technology and failed to grasp the manner in which markets actually work. There are six reasons why the media giants have blown any prospective competitors out of the Internet waters.

1. The giant media firms are willing to take losses on the Internet that would be absurd for any other investor to assume. For a Disney or Time Warner or Viacom to lose $200–$300 million annually on the Internet is a drop in the bucket, if it means their core activities worth tens of billions of dollars are protected down the road. As one media executive put it in *Advertising Age*, Internet "losses appear to be the key to the future." The media giants have to try to cover all their online bases until they can see how the Internet develops as a commercial medium. For any other investor, who is not protecting media assets worth $50–$100 billion, assuming such annual losses would be absurd and irrational. The same money could be spent pursuing some other aspect of the Internet (or economy writ large) and generate much larger returns with less risk.

2. The media giants have digital programming from their other ventures that they can plug into the Web at little extra cost. This, in itself, is a huge advantage over firms that have to create original content from scratch.

3. To generate an audience, the media giants can and do promote their websites incessantly on their traditional media holdings, to bring their audiences to their online outlets. By 1998, it was argued that the only way an Internet content provider could generate users was by buying advertising in the media giants' traditional media. Otherwise, an Internet website would get lost among the millions of other Web locations. As the editor-in-chief of MSNBC on the Internet put it, linking the website to the existing media activity "is the crux of

what we are talking about; it will help set us apart in a crowded market." Indeed, much of the TV advertising boom in 1999 is attributed to Internet firms spending wildly to draw attention to their Web activities. The media giants can do at nominal expense what any other Internet firm would have to pay hundreds of millions of dollars to accomplish.

Hot Brands and Deep Pockets

4. As the possessors of the hottest "brands," the media firms have the leverage to get premier locations from browser software makers, Internet Service Providers (ISPs), search engines and portals. The new Microsoft Internet Explorer 4.0 offers 250 highlighted channels, and the "plum positions" belong to Disney and Time Warner. Similar arrangements are taking place with Netscape and Pointcast. Indeed, the portals are eager to promote "Hollywoodesque programming" in the competition for users.

5. With their deep pockets, the media giants are aggressive investors in start-up Internet media companies. Some estimates have as much as one-half the venture capital for Internet content start-up companies coming from established media firms. The Tribune Company, for example, owns stakes in 15 Internet companies, including the portals AOL, Excite and iVillage, which targets women.

Some media giants, like Bertelsmann and Sony, have seemingly bypassed new acquisitions of traditional media to put nearly all their resources into expanding their Internet presence. GE's NBC arguably has taken this strategy the furthest. To cover all the bases, GE has invested over $2 billion in more than 20 Internet companies, in addition to NBC's own Web activities. "It wants to be wherever this thing takes off," an industry analyst said in *Electronic Media*. In sum, if some new company shows commercial promise, the media giants will be poised to capitalize upon it, not be buried by it.

6. To the extent that advertising develops on the Web, the media giants are positioned to seize most of these revenues. Online advertising amounted to $900 million in 1997, and some expect it to reach $5 billion by 2000. The media giants have long and close relationships with the advertising industry, and can and do get major advertisers to sponsor their on-

line ventures as a package deal when the advertisers buy spots on the media giants' traditional media. . . .

Taking Back Cyberspace

While the Internet is in many ways revolutionizing the way we lead our lives, it is a revolution that does not appear to include changing the identity and nature of those in power. Those who think the technology can produce a viable democratic public sphere by itself where policy has failed to do so are deluding themselves.

This does not mean that there will not be a vibrant, exciting and important noncommercial citizen's sector in cyberspace, open to all who veer far off the beaten path. For activists of all political stripes, the Web increasingly plays a central role in organizing and educational activities. But from its once lofty perch, this nonprofit and civic sector has been relegated to the distant margins of cyberspace; it is nowhere near the heart of the dominant commercial sector. And we should be careful not to extrapolate from the experience of activists what the Internet experience will look like for the bulk of the population.

In fact, as the corporate media domination of Internet "content" crystallizes, the claims of the Internet utopians are beginning to get downsized. We are probably going to hear less about how the Internet will invigorate media competition and more about how since anyone can start a website, we should all just shut up and be happy consumers. But, in the big scheme of things, having the ability to launch a website at a nominal expense is only slightly more compelling than saying we have no grounds of concern about monopoly newspapers because anyone can write up a newsletter and wave it in their front window or hand it out to their neighbors.

Viable websites for journalism and entertainment need resources and people who earn a living at producing them, precisely what the market has eliminated any chance of developing. Moreover, just having a zillion amateur websites may not be all that impressive. One expert estimates that over 80 percent of all websites fail to show up on any search engines, making them virtually impossible to find, and the situation may only get worse.

The moral of the story is clear: If we want a vibrant non-commercial and nonprofit sector on the Internet, in the near term it will require existing institutions like labor and progressive funders to subsidize such activities. In the long run, the key to democratizing the Internet as a medium will be to structurally change our media system to lower the power of Wall Street and Madison Avenue, and to increase the power of Main Street and every other street.

A media system chock full of new nonprofit, noncommercial and even small commercial entities would go a long way toward improving the Internet as a medium. This is something the American people have every right to do. The federal government created and subsidized the Internet for three decades before it was effectively privatized and opened to commercial domination—with zero public debate or press coverage—in the early 1990s. It is time to take it back.

"Online retailing turned out to be just as hard as off-line, if not harder. . . . Many success stories were artificially generated."

Internet Retailers Will Revert to Traditional Methods of Commerce

David Streitfeld

David Streitfeld reports in the following viewpoint that it is as difficult to sell products on the Internet as it is in traditional stores. When e-commerce first began, he explains, Internet companies thought they could grow quickly by spending vast amounts of money on marketing and by underselling the competition, which resulted in most online retailers going bankrupt. Streitfeld asserts that in the future, Internet companies will be successful only if they maintain a strong off-line presence and sell goods in a more traditional manner. David Streitfeld is a *Washington Post* staff writer.

As you read, consider the following questions:
1. According to Streitfeld, what are three clichés that have informed the marketing decisions of Internet retailers?
2. By what percentage did Amazon and Priceline shares fall in 2000, according to the author?
3. According to the author, what is "gain sharing"?

M ost new ventures collapse because they can't attract enough customers. The WebHouse Club, which used the Internet to sell discounted groceries, closed at least in part because it attracted too many.

"I was so happy to pay half-price for everything," says Hazel Walker, a legal secretary who lives in Fort Washington, Md. She discovered WebHouse in August 2000 and was an immediate convert. One week she bought $62.37 worth of groceries at her local supermarket but paid only $39.96.

"It seemed too good to be true," Walker says. "You know the grocery stores had to be getting the money they intended to make. And WebHouse only charged me this little fee—50 cents or so. I don't know how they did it."

A More Sober Era

It was too good to be true. WebHouse was basically making up the difference between what the grocer charged and what Walker paid. Do that for hundreds of thousands of customers and even an outfit as well funded as WebHouse will run out of cash and have to close, which it did in October 2000.

The failure of WebHouse, a highly publicized offshoot of one of the best-known Internet retailers, the airline-ticket seller Priceline.com, marks the end of the first stage of electronic commerce—the high-spirited, free-spending, deep-discounting, we're-making-it-up-as-we-go-along age.

Now comes the more sober era, one that analysts say will be dominated by brand names people know and love from the off-line world. The home page for the Yahoo shopping network, for example, currently features a dozen sites, all but one from such familiar outfits as Brooks Brothers, Clinique and Barnes & Noble. The 12th, eLuxury, is a new company but largely owned by LVMH, one of the world's largest luxury-goods operations.

Even the biggest Internet retailer, Amazon.com, has reached off-line. After a troubled attempt to sell toys by itself in 1999, Amazon struck a deal with Toys R Us for a joint site. Such hybrids are expected to become increasingly popular.

If Web companies no longer attract customers by essentially giving away money, like WebHouse, they'll have to appeal with service. Live chat lines, where potential customers can ask questions through their computers, are no longer rare. New middlemen will soon spring up to act as agents for consumers, working to secure the best deal for them.

All this will help e-commerce continue to grow. Sales are projected to hit $29.3 billion in 2000, up 75 percent over 1999, according to an estimate by the Gartner Group. But that sum is still dwarfed by the total retail market, more than $750 billion. In the euphoria of 1998 and '99, that fact was often overlooked.

"For a while, people were talking about the disintermediation of distributors, the removal of inefficient outlets and the rationalization of retailing," says Ken Berryman, a consultant with McKinsey & Co., a management consulting firm. "But in most retailing categories, that's not going to happen. The economics have changed a bit, but they haven't been upended."

Marketing Clichés

What have been upended are the supposed rules for doing business on the Internet, many of which hardened into clichés without ever being proved effective. The most repeated rule was Get Big Fast: Get as many customers as possible by whatever means, which usually involved selling products at a loss. Once you had a group of loyal customers, you could then boost prices or employ more complicated strategy to raise profit margins. In theory this might work; in practice, most companies just ran out of money to give away.

To get noticed by all those potential customers, companies were urged to spend wildly on marketing. This was the Brand Yourself cliché. If there are 10 companies selling pet food online, the argument went, customers will flock to the one they've at least dimly heard of.

Brand creation in the physical world usually involves years of work to build a popular, distinctive product. Dot-coms were generally selling generic material—books, tapes and so on—which made brand-building even more difficult. One of the few successful brands to be created in cyberspace is Amazon.com, and it's debatable whether customers identify it with anything except its core book business.

Finally there was the notion that Clicks Beat Bricks. The

off-line retailers weren't supposed to understand the Internet, and for a long time they didn't. Now they do—so much so that several venture capitalists said they couldn't think of a single "pure play" Internet retailer (with the exception of the auction site eBay) that they believed would survive and thrive.

"The Internet is not a business model," says Chris Lochhead, chief marketing officer of the consulting company Scient. "Being an electronic catalogue is not enough."

A Frenzy on the Downside

Selling on the Internet was supposed to be easy. Everything would speed along by the network effect: Happy users would tell other users, each of whom would tell more users. The whole world, or at least those parts with access to the Internet, would know. The process would be frictionless—and free.

"Entrepreneurs saw the success of some of the business models like eBay, which were truly new and did depend on network effects," says Berryman, the McKinsey & Co. consultant. "They thought the same thing applied to online retail. The truth is, there isn't much of a network effect with online retailers, just as there isn't much with off-line retail."

Online retailing turned out to be just as hard as off-line, if not harder, analysts say. Many success stories were artificially generated. "A lot of this was driven because they were giving stuff away," says venture capitalist Art Berliner. "That was a great deal for the consumer. It was not so great for the companies."

It's a conclusion that the stock market is echoing. Electronic retailers that didn't sell shares to the public before the market tumble in March and April 2000 were the first to lose. Many of them have run out of cash and shut down, including such operations as Clickmango.com, BBQ.com, Living.com, Value America, Homewarehouse.com, Craftshop.com, Toysmart.com, Redrocket.com and Violet.com. Two weeks ago, in October 2000, a golf-equipment site, Chipshot.com, filed for bankruptcy protection. It had raised, and spent, more than $50 million.

Many of those who did make it to the public markets, such as Pets.com, the pharmacy PlanetRx.com and the sporting-goods retailer Fogdog, now trade for pennies a share. Even leaders such as Amazon and Priceline have fallen 80 percent.

"People are unable to figure out the real value of these companies. So every day their value is getting lower," says venture capitalist Erik Straser. "Last year there was a frenzy on the upside with these stocks. Now there's a frenzy on the downside."

The Need to Be Different

The problem with many of the retailers that sprang up on the Internet is that they had control over such a small part of their product's life. They didn't make the goods. They didn't necessarily ship their products—that was contracted out. They probably couldn't repair them or accept returns. Essentially all they did, whether the product was dog food, makeup, hammers, CDs or DVDs, was solicit and take orders.

The strategy was often to create customer loyalty by selling at rock-bottom prices. After all, a dot-com site didn't have a store with an expensive lease, or any clerks or cashiers. It could operate more cheaply and thus sell more cheaply.

But it turned out that all that marketing cost a lot. So did the programmers to maintain the site, any of whom earned more than four retail clerks combined. So did the logistics of distribution. In the end, the Internet is only marginally cheaper, if at all.

A Mad Mall

The Internet is an infinite mall where you need a shopping directory to find the (flawed) shopping directory, where businesses lurk behind pillars and in attic spaces, where stores open and close every second of every day. Most shoppers become familiar with a tiny corner of this mad mall, then hope and pray that nothing happens to destroy what few landmarks they recognize.

Paul Kedrosky, *Wall Street Journal*, November 23, 1998.

That makes it even more important to be different. "The question for an online company is: Is it part of something that couldn't be done before?" says Straser, a partner with Mohr, Davidow Ventures. "Yahoo passes that test, and so does eBay. Amazon doesn't. Wal-Mart is a pretty good substitute for Amazon."

A retailer that Straser believes has a promising future is Half.com, which brokers material between buyers and sellers like eBay, but at fixed prices. Half.com, which was recently bought by eBay for $300 million, takes a 15 percent commission on each sale.

Half.com is on the leading edge of the second generation of online retailers. Another strategy for this group will be the technique known as gain sharing. A consumer wants to buy, say, a mountain bike. Instead of going to a sporting-goods site, he appoints someone as his representative. This individual or electronic site helps the consumer find a seller and then negotiates on his behalf. The consumer is charged a percentage of the amount he saves.

"Then they'll start wrapping a bundle of value-added services around it," says Phil Anderson, director of the Glassmeyer/McNamee Center for Digital Strategies at Dartmouth College. "So I buy a lawn mower for you. How about if I also contract with someone to sharpen the blades twice a year?" Or even arrange for someone to come over and use the mower to cut the lawn?

"This is where shopping is going to go next," Anderson says. "Call it assisted shopping. It's where you know the outcome you want, but you don't know how to do it. So I'm going to sell you the outcome."

Venture capitalists are far more stingy now about turning over $5 million to anyone who gives them a convincing pitch about a new e-commerce company. But that doesn't mean that new companies aren't being started. Entrepreneurs are just doing it the old-fashioned way: with their own money, in their living rooms. Get Big Slow has replaced Get Big Fast.

Sneetch Success

A case in point is Sneetch.com, a DVD, game and audio-book retailer started in January by two friends who worked at Disneyland. Sales so far are an estimated $500,000. More impressively, the founders say it's profitable. This is achieved by having low overhead: two employees, no office space, no advertising, no interest on loans. Total invested capital was about $2,000.

"When we were starting, we were told every single day how easy it would be to submit a business plan to a venture capitalist and get money," Sean Lundgren says.

"We'd have been really happy for the first two or three months," says Todd Livdahl. "But right now, in October 2000, we'd be stressing our butts off, saying 'This sucks.' We would owe a ton of money to someone."

Sneetch began as one of 12,000 merchants on Yahoo's shopping site. For $100 a month in "rent," it could open a "store" and list a maximum of 50 items for sale. One of them was the newly released unrated version of the movie "American Pie," which was the first thing anyone ordered from Sneetch. To fulfill the order, Lundgren and Livdahl drove to local stores, finally finding the DVD after three hours. "Lost money on that order," Livdahl says with a laugh. Yahoo liked Sneetch so much that they were invited to become a featured shopping partner, which was somewhat equivalent to an extra in a movie being chosen as the star. That lucky break gave Lundgren and Livdahl the exposure and sales they needed to develop a full-scale Web site.

What Sneetch is trying to do is use the Internet to its advantage. "Customers don't know that we're not a major company," Lundgren says. "We're competing with Tower Records, Big Star, Barnes & Noble."

Sneetch hired another company to process orders. It never touches the tapes it sells. Since there are only the two of them, a sudden influx of orders could kill the company faster than a sudden drought. To get an office, they'll need to take on an investor and thus give up some of the control they prize.

But at least they're not crashing and burning, like Gazoontite. In October 2000, the San Francisco firm—started early in 1999 to develop a Web site devoted to all sorts of better-breathing products, from chemical-free cotton pillow covers to anti-allergen dust spray—filed for bankruptcy protection.

Gazoontite seemed to be the sort of thing the Internet was designed for: Anyone who had respiratory problems could find help there. The site was well designed, with message boards, a nurse to answer questions and information on how to create a healthy house. It wasn't surprising that venture capitalists gave Gazoontite $26.5 million. All that cash is gone now.

Strangely, the company's five retail stores remain open. Located in San Francisco, New York City, Long Island, Orange County, Calif., and the Chicago area, stores were opened simply "to build brand awareness" for the Web site, then-chief executive Soon-Chart Yu said. The stores turned profitable, which the Web site never did. So now things have come full circle. In a development no e-commerce analyst would have been bold enough to predict 18 months ago, visitors to the Gazoontite.com site who try to order a product are told, "to purchase this . . . please visit one of our retail stores."

*"Telephone service is moving off the
traditional telephone system, on which voice
communications dominate, and onto the
Internet, which it will share with . . . a
near-infinite variety of other data."*

Traditional Phones Will Be Replaced by the Internet

Michael A. Hiltzik

In the following viewpoint, Michael A. Hiltzik reports that
voice communications can be transmitted over the Internet
more cheaply and efficiently than over traditional phone
lines. He explains that traditional phone carriers such as
AT&T have begun to invest in Internet calling technology
in response to their customers' demand for lower prices and
additional services. The transition to Internet calling will
likely be slow because the phone system is more familiar, reliable, and ubiquitous, but many technology experts predict
that Internet calling will one day replace traditional calling.
Michael A. Hiltzik is a staff writer for the *Los Angeles Times*.

As you read, consider the following questions:
1. According to Hiltzik, what are "digital packets"?
2. How long do most forecasters predict Internet calling
   will have to coexist with traditional calling, according to
   the author?
3. According to Hiltzik, what technologies have been
   developed to improve the quality of Internet calls?

The city of Silute, Lithuania, with a population of 22,000 and a location three hours from the national capital, is an unlikely place from which to foment a revolution.

That's particularly true of the one Stepas Kairys carries on simply by staying on the telephone for hours at a time.

For the equivalent of $10 a month, Kairys, a 49-year-old basketball coach who has helped place 60 Lithuanian players on U.S. high school and college teams, gets to make unlimited calls to the United States. His calls to European countries often cost a tenth of standard rates.

The only sacrifice—a minor one, he says—is that he has to make his calls from a headphone-and-mike arrangement connected to his personal computer, which enables the calls to move not over conventional phone lines, but the Internet.

"I can't imagine my life without it," he says.

Telephone Revolution

Kairys is a pioneer, but the rest of the world is not far behind him. Telephone service is moving off the traditional telephone system, on which voice communications dominate, and onto the Internet, which it will share with Web pages, video and music transmissions, and a near-infinite variety of other data.

As that change unfolds, a tidal wave of innovation will swamp the traditional telephone business—and will likely lead to lower prices and better features for consumers.

The transition is already underway. Many international calls already travel, at last partially, over the Internet, and dozens of small companies have sprung up to offer free or cut-rate dialing for long-distance customers by bypassing the conventional phone system.

The big telephone companies whose franchise has depended on traditional phone technology are taking notice. "This is coming at us whether we want it to or not," says Cathy-Ann Martine, president of the international carrier services unit of Concert, a joint venture of AT&T and British Telecom that will operate high-speed Internet telephone services in 60 countries, including China and Japan, by mid-2001. "It's a freight train."

Moving voice calls to the Internet also opens the doors for

non-telephone companies to offer phone service—leading to more competition that may also benefit consumers. "The idea of Internet service provider America Online as a telephone company is not really farfetched," Martine says.

Cheap and Convenient

In simple terms, Internet telephones work by breaking up the sounds of callers' voices into a stream of digital "packets" and piping them onto digital networks at high speed. Because they share these networks with packets carrying Web-page data, music and video, they travel at much lower cost than a traditional voice call, which monopolizes a single circuit linking the callers.

The benefits to consumers are already becoming clear. It is not only that ordinary calls can be transmitted cheaply. Once linked inextricably to a computer network, the telephone itself becomes a lot smarter.

"What's so powerful about the Internet is that your phone isn't a black box, but a Pentium III piece of hardware," says Bruce Maxwell, vice president of strategy and planning for Firetalk Communications, which allows subscribers to hold phone conversations via their computers for free.

That means phone services can become as flexible and imaginative as computer programs.

"We have a friend in London who's very time-insensitive and keeps calling us at 5 a.m.," says Jeff Pulver, a market analyst who sponsors several "Voice on the Net" industry conferences every year. "I'd love to have a 'Do Not Disturb' sign on my phone that tells him the Pulvers are sleeping now, but if you want to wake them, dial 1. Or a distinctive in-box that answers 'Hi, Mom,' if Mom calls from her home number.

"When my [6-year-olds] turn 10, they'll have their own [computerized] answering machines. There will be callers who get busy signals, callers who get voicemail, and callers who get through."

Enhanced Service

Routing calls over the Internet will give service providers new opportunities to offer customers cheap conference calling, video calling and integrated voice and e-mail. Some of those services have been available for years from conventional phone companies, but at prices that make them inaccessible to most users. At least one company, EVoice, already offers a free service that accepts voice messages left on your home or business phone and allows you to retrieve them, via digital audio files, from any Internet Web browser.

Others see a day when anyone can be reached by the same phone number no matter where he or she is in the world, just as one can read one's e-mail from almost any computer. That's because inside one's telephone will be a unique code that identifies it to the worldwide network the moment it is plugged into a network.

Changing Numbers

Internet phone traffic in minutes and as a percentage of total phone traffic.

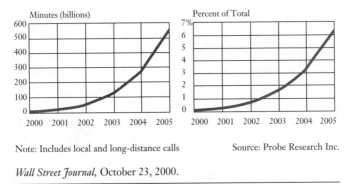

Note: Includes local and long-distance calls   Source: Probe Research Inc.

Wall Street Journal, October 23, 2000.

"There are probably more applications than anyone has even thought about," says Greg Braden, the head of telephony services at MediaOne, the large cable system operator that provides consumer phone service over its network in Culver City, California, and elsewhere in the country. "The result will change the very nature of what a telephone call is."

The merging of voice and data may also improve the Web-surfing experience.

"Everything happening on the Web today will [soon] have voice attached," says David Greenblatt, chief operating officer of Net2Phone, which provides long-distance service at cut rates over its data network. "In e-commerce it's no secret that 70% of [shoppers] enter the site and leave [without buying anything]. What you have is a Nordstrom's without employees. But what if you had someone there telling you how something fit, or how it'll wash and wear? Every place is better with a human interface."

Change Is Slow

As with any heavily anticipated technological revolution, how soon these applications will actually materialize is still an open question. The traditional phone system is ubiquitous and familiar—and the beneficiary of billions of dollars of investment over the years. Even the most liberal forecasters expect Internet telephony to coexist with the Ma Bell variety for at least the next 10 years.

"It takes a long time to unseat a technology," Greenblatt says. "There will always be pieces and stragglers who will never go."

The traditional phone system has another advantage over alternatives: Its robust dependability. Americans have come to expect their phones to work 99.999% of the time—the so-called "five nines" standard. As anyone knows who has cursed a crashed computer or catatonic Internet connection, data systems don't yet come close to that mark.

"Data networks aren't known for their rock-solid reliability," says Michael Van Norman, technology and development manager for University of California, Los Angeles's (UCLA) communications technology services department, which manages a system of more than 30,000 phones on campus and at UCLA Medical Center.

"There may be some areas where the phones absolutely cannot go down," he says, "like the hospital or our police and fire departments. So until these issues are worked out, we don't see [Internet telephones] as a replacement."

Communications engineers expect these and other issues to be ironed out fairly quickly, however.

"Ten years from now there won't be a phone call that doesn't go over the Internet," says Thomas Evslin, a former Microsoft and AT&T executive who is chairman and chief executive of ITXC, a company that wholesales Internet minutes to telephone carriers.

If this shift is to be successful, it will have to be invisible to the average phone user. But it will represent a crossroads for the industry.

Joining the Revolution

Phone companies are already suffering from an elemental shift in the public's telephone habits. Barely 10 years ago, most people relied for almost all their calls on their monopoly local phone company and a single long-distance company; on the road the choice was a pay phone or nothing.

But that sort of enforced loyalty is a thing of the past. Even at home one can choose from a vast array of long-distance providers—one's regular service, or a "dial-around" service using the 10-10 prefix, or a phone card available from any of dozens of providers, including some that transmit the calls over the Internet, or a handy cell phone. For many homeowners the basis of the choice is simply price.

The impact on traditional carriers has been dramatic. AT&T, the nation's largest long-distance carrier, in May 2000 sharply cut its estimates of revenue growth in part because consumers are "moving from basic wired long distance to wireless and Internet services at greater rates" than anticipated, in the words of its chairman, C. Michael Armstrong. "These forces have accelerated in recent months."

AT&T had already taken steps to join a revolution it knows it can't beat. As leader of an investment consortium, the company in March 2000 paid $1.4 billion for a one-third stake in Net2Phone, the largest Internet phone company, with an option to purchase overall control.

This is happening while IP, or Internet Protocol, telephony still accounts for a tiny fraction of all phone traffic. While 476 million minutes of conversation and fax traffic was carried by voice over IP, or VOIP, networks in 1998, the world's long-distance carriers handled more than 880 billion minutes, according to a study by the investment firm of Piper Jaffray Inc.

But many communications experts believe the trend will build. "We are trying to get to VOIP in the core of our network as fast as we can," says Kathleen Earley, president of AT&T's data and information arm, "because the savings are enormous in getting rid of the legacy [traditional] networks."

The reasons derive from several historic changes in telecommunications traffic: The volume of data is steadily overtaking that of voice on the world's networks. Data traffic has exceeded voice traffic on U.S. long-distance networks since 1998, thanks to the growth of the Internet, and will pass voice on most other components of the system in 2000.

Parallel Freeway Systems

As the relative role of voice diminishes, it makes more sense to require that spoken conversations and digital data share a single network, rather than allowing voice to claim a huge portion of the nation's copper wiring for itself. Anything else would be as wasteful as building parallel freeway systems; say, one for Mazda Miatas and one for all other vehicles.

"Today you have two networks," says Noam Bardin, the chief executive of the telecommunications company DeltaThree. "One does everything, and the other does only voice. That means the [phone network] has no real technological reason to be around in the future."

That's especially true because transmitting data by Internet protocol is much cheaper than transmitting voice by electronic pulse, the traditional method.

Think of the traditional phone network as a huge bundle of discrete lines, like individual coast-to-coast spaghetti strands. Every conversation ties up one of those strands for its entire duration regardless of whether the parties are speaking, silent, or keeping each other on hold.

Phone bills have long been billed by duration and distance because of this architecture: The longer the call and the farther apart its participants, the greater the demand on a finite resource.

Not so when the freight is digital data. Data transmissions— say, the images and text comprising a Web page—are broken up into individual packets of digital bits before being shot onto the Internet, the backbone of which is not a bundle of discrete circuits but copper wires, coaxial cables, and fiber-optic lines making up a vast lattice of interlocking arms and branches.

Each packet traverses its own path, getting routed around

traffic jams when necessary, until all arrive at their destination generally out of order and out of sync, like the violinists in a grade-school orchestra. At that point they are reassembled in proper order so the Web page can appear on your screen.

Therein lies the opportunity for voice on the Internet—and the impediment. Broken up into packets, voice can travel the information freeway like any other data, with time and distance reduced to irrelevancies. That's why some Internet telephone companies can offer PC-to-phone calling services for pennies a minute or even for free.

A Round-Trip Detour to the Moon

On the other hand, voice requires much more precision than raw data. The delays and misroutings that commonly afflict data packets on the Internet barely matter when they are carrying text or images, because they can be retransmitted or ignored without noticeable degradation of the end product.

But the same problems render conversations unintelligible. And that's why many of those free Internet conversations sound like bad cellular calls and are at worst interrupted by pauses and static that make it sound as though each person's words have made a round-trip detour to the moon.

Some of these glitches are already on the way to being solved by a combination of network and software improvements. Several start-up companies have invested in private fiber-optic data networks that circumvent the public Internet backbones and avoid their bottlenecks. Meanwhile, manufacturers like Cisco Systems have devised switches, known as routers, that distinguish between voice and data packets and give the former priority, thus cutting down on transmission delays.

Voice quality is an area of critical research, for Internet telephone companies understand that to succeed, sound on their networks will have to be nearly indistinguishable from that of traditional networks. That's especially because their price advantage is rapidly fading as the cost plummets for standard long-distance calls.

Periodical Bibliography

The following articles have been selected to supplement the diverse views presented in this chapter. Addresses are provided for periodicals not indexed in the *Readers' Guide to Periodical Literature*, the *Alternative Press Index*, the *Social Sciences Index*, or the *Index to Legal Periodicals and Books*.

Ian Austen	"Meet the New Web. Same as the Old Web," *New York Times*, September 28, 2000.
Rajiv Chandrasekaran	"Repaving the Information Superhighway," *Washington Post*, October 20, 1997.
Eric C. Evarts	"'Father of the Internet' Reflects on His Creation: An Interview with Vinton Cerf," *Christian Science Monitor*, October 30, 1996.
Andrew Hammer	"Talkin' About a Revolution: How Being Online Has Changed Our Lives," *Democratic Left*, 1999.
Robert D. Hormats	"The Technologies of Freedom," *Wall Street Journal*, December 22, 1999.
John Horvath	"The New World Cyberspace Order," *Toward Freedom*, September/October 1997.
Raymond K. Neff	"Teleworld," *World & I*, May 2000. Available from 3600 New York Ave. NE, Washington, DC 20002.
Charles Piller	"E-Bonding Via Voice on the Web," *Los Angeles Times*, September 29, 1999. Available from Times Mirror Square, Los Angeles, CA 90053.
Frank Rich	"We All Pass Go. They Collect $200," *New York Times*, June 3, 2000.
Robert J. Samuelson	"Just How Important Is the Internet?" *Newsweek*, January 20, 2000.

Glossary

ARPANET   One of the world's first computer networks, now defunct, created by the Department of Defense's Advanced Research Projects Agency in the 1970s.

bandwidth   The width of the conduit that transmits data over the **Internet.** The higher the bandwidth, the faster data can be transmitted.

browser   Software that enables the user to view and navigate the **World Wide Web.**

bulletin board   A computer system where users log on and share messages with other users.

chat room   An online environment where users can interact with each other in **real time** by typing messages and sending them over the **Internet.**

cookie   A small file left on computers by websites a user has visited. Cookies are used to gather information about users' **Internet** surfing habits.

cyberspace   The virtual space created by the **Internet.** The term was coined by author William Gibson in *Neuromancer.*

database   A multi-user collection of organized information.

digital   A device or method that uses discrete electrical variations to encode, process, or carry binary (zero or one) signals for sound, video, computer data, or other information.

domain name   The name assigned to a unique **Internet** protocol address, such as www.congress.gov.

download   To receive a file or program from another computer.

encryption   The process of converting information into secret code; only those with the right key can translate it.

FAQ   Frequently Asked Question.

fiber optics   A high-speed data transmission channel made of high-purity glass strands sealed within an opaque tube. Because it uses light as a carrier, wave transmission via fiber optics is much faster and more powerful than via metal wire channels such as coaxial cable.

flame   To post an insulting message against another Internet user.

hacker   Slang for a computer expert who writes programs and/or breaks into networks.

HTML   Hypertext Markup Language. A convention of codes

that makes information accessible on the **World Wide Web.** HTML codes allow Web browsers to read such information.

hyperlink   Connections between one piece of information and another on the **World Wide Web.**

Internet   The largest international computer network, made up of scores of smaller networks linked together by international protocols.

ISP   Internet Service Provider. ISPs such as America Online provide a portal through which users can access the **Internet.**

modem   A device that allows a computer's digital signals to transmit over telephone lines.

multimedia   Any document that uses multiple forms of communication, such as text, audio, and/or video.

netizen   Slang for a citizen of the **Internet;** an **Internet** user.

newsgroup   A bulletin board focused on a particular topic. **Usenet** is a system hosting many different newsgroups.

protocol   A standardized method of transmitting information, such as the **Internet** protocol.

real time   User-to-user interactions that occur instantaneously.

server   A computer or program that allows other computers to access information stored on it.

spam   Junk e-mail used for advertising purposes.

Unix   An operating system developed in the 1970s that was popular among programmers but was difficult for others to use.

upload   To send a file or program to another computer.

URL   Uniform Resource Locator. The method of addressing data based on the name of the server where the site's files are stored, the file's directory path, and its file name.

Usenet   A "newsgroup," or discussion group, that is accessed via the **Internet.**

venture capital   Money provided by outside investors to finance the creation of small businesses.

website   Location of a server on the **Internet** where a specific entity such as a university has stored files for users to download. Websites can be located via their Uniform Resource Locators (URLs) or via a search engine.

World Wide Web   A collection of millions of websites on the Internet devoted to specific companies, government entities, individuals, organizations, and schools.

For Further Discussion

Chapter 1

1. Janna Malamud Smith supports her argument that the Internet helps people stay connected by providing examples of her son and her chatting with distant friends online. On the other hand, Douglas Groothuis contends that online communication—such as that extolled by Smith—cannot provide the trust and human interaction necessary to build meaningful relationships. Describe a deep friendship that you enjoy, listing the specific qualities that make it meaningful and enduring. In your opinion, can such friendships be developed and sustained over the Internet? Why or why not?

2. Anthony G. Wilhelm uses a U.S. Department of Commerce study—which found that affluent people are more likely to own computers than those at the lowest income level—to argue that unequal access to the Internet harms society. However, Eric Cohen criticizes the way Wilhelm and others use the Commerce study, contending that they exaggerate the extent of the "digital divide" by ignoring statistics that show that the digital divide is narrowing. In your opinion, how do Cohen's assertions affect the cogency of Wilhelm's argument? Examine the rest of Wilhelm's evidence and explain whether or not his omission of positive Commerce study findings seriously undermines his conclusion.

3. Stacia Brown claims that Internet hate groups are a serious problem. Conversely, Charles Platt maintains that there are fewer hate groups operating on the Internet than many watchdog groups contend, and suggests that their websites might even serve a useful purpose in providing a forum for hateful views to be debated. In your opinion, do hate groups on the Internet pose a threat to society by encouraging intolerance, or do they benefit society by exposing racist, homophobic, and anti-Semitic views to criticism?

4. D. Douglas Rehman uses his personal experience as an Internet pedophile investigator to argue that pedophilia on the Internet is a serious problem. James R. Kincaid—a professor at the University of Southern California—supports his argument that Internet pedophiles are not a threat by pointing to a lack of evidence that they are. Furthermore, Kincaid argues that investigators— such as Rehman—actually trap men into engaging in illegal behavior that they would not otherwise have engaged in. Which author do you think has better credentials to comment on the Internet pe-

dophile issue? Which author makes the most convincing argument and why?

Chapter 2

1. Bruce O. Barker provides a list of specific ways the Internet can be used in the classroom to make his case that the Internet can improve education. Conversely, David Kushner provides an example of one high school that uses the Internet to make his point that the technology does not improve education. In your opinion, which author uses the most convincing evidence to construct his argument? Explain your answer.

2. In your experience, what are some of the problems that can make it difficult for students to get a good education? Are these problems within the school system, society, the home, the individual, or a combination of these? Do you think that using the Internet in the classroom can provide solutions to these problems? Please explain.

3. Lynne Lamberg argues that the Internet can improve health care by providing people with networks that enable them to discuss medical problems with one another. Conversely, the Public Citizen Health Research Group contends that the Internet can harm health care by providing inaccurate and misleading medical information. In your opinion, what would be the best way to utilize the Internet in order to find information on and support for a health condition such as drug addiction or anorexia? What nonelectronic sources could a person use to supplement Internet sources?

Chapter 3

1. Rutt Bridges argues that government regulation of personal data collection on the Internet may be required in order to protect users' privacy. However, Declan McCullagh contends that the government is more likely than online merchants to invade your privacy. In your opinion, can online companies be trusted to protect your privacy? Or would you feel more secure knowing that the government was regulating the use of cookies and other devices for collecting data online? Please explain your answer.

2. Robert Flores refers to legal cases and existing statutes to support his argument that laws regulating pornography on the Internet should be enforced in order to protect children. Keith Wade cites examples of nongovernmental solutions such as filters to argue that government regulation of pornography on the Internet is not the most effective method of protecting children.

Based on the evidence each author provides, which do you think makes the most convincing argument and why?

3. Byron Dorgan asserts that current law requires all online purchases to be taxed, and claims that these laws should be simplified so that consumers and merchants will comply with them. Lawrence W. Reed maintains that Internet commerce should not be taxed because it would impede the Internet's growth. Do you believe Dorgan when he claims that the law already requires Internet commerce to be taxed? Why or why not? Does the fact that Reed never mentions that law undermine his argument? Please explain.

4. Randall E. Stross predicts that unregulated exchange of free music over the Internet will harm record companies and others who deal in intellectual property. However, Phyllis Schlafly contends that swapping free music online is legal under the fair-use application of copyright law. If you recorded a CD or wrote a software program, would you care if it was shared for free over the Internet? Do you think that most of the creators of intellectual property need financial compensation to continue with their work, or would they continue to create just for the satisfaction of doing so?

Chapter 4

1. Kunda Dixit argues that the Internet will benefit only those who can afford computers—such as the affluent in developed nations—while Matthew R. Estabrook claims that the Internet has the capacity to empower all individuals. In your opinion, will people who cannot afford Internet access be at a decided disadvantage over those who can? Discuss specific advantages that the Internet provides when formulating your answer.

2. Jennifer L. Schenker explains that the Internet will make possible future conveniences such as sensors that can regulate the temperature of your home to suit your particular preferences. Examine Schenker's article and comment on the significance of the technological advances she describes. Do you think they will improve the human condition, or do you believe people would be helped more by other kinds of technological advances? If so, describe them.

3. David Streitfeld claims that Internet retailers are reverting to traditional methods of commerce—such as having a physical store in addition to their website—in order to stay in business. Compare the experience of shopping on the Internet with shop-

ping in a mall. List the advantages and disadvantages of both and explain which method you think is best.

4. Michael A. Hiltzik reports that the Internet will replace traditional phones. In your opinion, how eagerly do most people adopt new technology, especially when it replaces technology such as phones to which they are accustomed? Please explain your answer by discussing specific technologies that have been replaced by newer technologies in recent times.

Organizations to Contact

The editors have compiled the following list of organizations concerned with the issues debated in this book. The descriptions are derived from materials provided by the organizations. All have publications or information available for interested readers. The list was compiled on the date of publication of the present volume; names, addresses, and phone numbers may change. Be aware that many organizations take several weeks or longer to respond to inquiries, so allow as much time as possible.

Canada's Coalition for Public Information (CPI-CCIP)
PO Box 726, Adelaide St., Toronto, Ontario M5C 2J8 Canada
(416) 260-8336 • fax: (416) 593-0249
e-mail: cip@web.net • website: www.canarie.ca/cpi/index/html
CPI-CCIP was founded in 1993 by the Ontario Library Association to ensure that the developing information infrastructure in Canada serves the public interest, focuses on human communication, and provides universal access to information. It is a coalition of organizations, public interest groups, and individuals that provides an effective grassroots voice for promoting and facilitating access to the benefits of telecomputing technology to maximize participation in a knowledge society and economy.

Center for Civic Networking (CCN)
PO Box 65272, Washington, DC 20037
(202) 362-3831 • fax: (202) 986-2539
e-mail: ccn-info@civicnet.org • website: www.civicnet.org
CCN is a nonprofit organization dedicated to applying information technology and infrastructure for the public good, particularly to improve access to information and the delivery of government services, to broaden citizen participation in government, and to stimulate economic and community development. It conducts policy research and analysis and consults with government and nonprofit organizations. The center publishes the weekly *CivicNet Gazette*.

Center for Democracy and Technology (CDT)
1634 Eye St. NW, Suite 1100, Washington, DC 20006
(202) 637-9800 • fax: (202) 637-0968
e-mail: info@cdt.org • website: www.cdt.org
The mission of CDT is to develop public policy solutions that advance constitutional civil liberties and democratic values in new computer and communications media. Pursuing its mission through pol-

icy research, public education, and coalition building, the center works to increase citizens' privacy and the public's control over the use of personal information held by government and other institutions. Its publications include issue briefs, policy papers, and *CDT-Policy Posts*, an online, occasional publication that covers issues regarding the civil liberties of those using the information highway.

Center for Media Education (CME)
2120 L St. NW, Suite 200, Washington, DC 20037
(202) 331-7833
e-mail: cme@cme.org • website: www.cme.org

CME is a nonprofit public interest group concerned with media and telecommunications issues, such as educational television for children, universal public access to the information highway, and the development and ownership of information services. Its projects include the Campaign for Kids TV, which seeks to improve children's education; the Future of Media, concerning the information highway; and the Telecommunications Policy Roundtable of monthly meetings of nonprofit organizations. CME publishes the monthly newsletter *InfoActive: Telecommunications Monthly for Nonprofits*.

CyberAngels
PO Box 516, Mineola, TX 75773
website: www.cyberangels.org

CyberAngels helps law enforcement protect computer users—especially children—from stalkers and online predators. One of the organization's main objectives is to locate and report child pornography, which is illegal. CyberAngel's Net Patrol has helped law enforcement make arrests of online criminals.

Electronic Frontier Foundation (EFF)
PO Box 170190, San Francisco, CA 94117
(415) 668-7171 • fax: (415) 668-7007
e-mail: eff@eff.org • website: www.eff.org

EFF is an organization of students and other individuals that aims to promote a better understanding of telecommunications issues. It fosters awareness of civil liberties issues arising from advancements in computer-based communications media and supports litigation to preserve, protect, and extend First Amendment rights in computing and telecommunications technologies. EFF's publications include *Building the Open Road*, *Crime and Puzzlement*, the quarterly newsletter *Networks and Policy*, the biweekly electronic newsletter *EFFector Online*, and online bulletins and publications, including *First Amendment in Cyberspace*.

Electronic Privacy Information Center (EPIC)
1718 Connecticut Ave. NW, Suite 200, Washington, DC 20009
(202) 483-1140 • fax: (202) 483-1248
e-mail: info@epic.org • website: www.epic.org
EPIC is an organization that advocates the public's right to electronic privacy. It sponsors educational and research programs, compiles statistics, and conducts litigation. Its publications include the biweekly electronic newsletter *EPIC Alert* and online reports.

HateWatch
955 Massachusetts Ave., Suite 141, Cambridge, MA 02139-3180
(617) 876-3796
website: www.hatewatch.org
HateWatch is a web-based educational resource and organization that works to combat the evolving problem of online bigotry. Originally a Harvard Law School Library web page, the project grew too large and needed a more activist-oriented organization. HateWatch monitors hate groups on the Internet and is a leader in the fight for civil rights and social justice.

Institute for Global Communications (IGC)
PO Box 29904, San Francisco, CA 94129-0904
(415) 561-6100 • fax: (415) 561-6101
e-mail: support@igc.apc.org
The institute provides computer networking services for international communications dedicated to environmental preservation, peace, and human rights. IGC networks include EcoNet, ConflictNet, LaborNet, and PeaceNet. It publishes the monthly newsletter *NetNews*.

Internet Society
11150 Sunset Hills Rd., Suite 100, Reston, VA 90190-5321
(703) 326-9880 • fax: (703) 326-9881
e-mail: isoc@isoc.org • website: www.isoc.org
A group of technologists, developers, educators, researchers, government representatives, and businesspeople, the Internet Society supports the development and dissemination of standards for the Internet and works to ensure global cooperation and coordination for the Internet and related Internet-working technologies and applications. It publishes the bimonthly magazine *On the Internet*.

Office of the Vice President
Communications Office, Old Executive Office Bldg., Room 272, Washington, DC 20501
(202) 456-7035 • fax: (202) 456-2685
website: www.whitehouse.gov

The White House in 1994 unveiled a program called "Welcome to the White House: An Interactive Citizens' Handbook," which is accessible on the World Wide Web. The program provides a single point of access to all electronic government information available on the Internet. Accessible material includes detailed information about cabinet-level and independent agencies and commissions, a subject-searchable index of federal information, and "hotlinks" to related areas of interest.

SafeSurf
1304 Newbury Rd., Unit E, Newbury Park, CA 91320
(805) 499-9160
e-mail: safesurf@safesurf.com • website: www.safesurf.com

The goal of SafeSurf is to prevent children from accessing adult material—including pornography—on the Internet. It maintains that standards must be implemented on the Internet to protect children. SafeSurf reviews entertainment products such as children's computer games and awards a seal of excellence to exceptional products. The organization publishes the quarterly newsletter *SafeSurf News*.

Simon Wiesenthal Center
1399 South Roxbury, Los Angeles, CA 90035
(800) 900-9036
website: www.wiesenthal.org

The organization is an international center for Holocaust remembrance, the defense of human rights and the Jewish people. The Simon Wiesenthal Center works to fight bigotry and anti-Semitism and pursues an active agenda related to contemporary issues. The organization publishes *Response* magazine.

Southern Poverty Law Center
400 Washington Ave., Montgomery, AL 36104
website: www.splcenter.org

The Southern Poverty Law Center is a nonprofit organization that combats hate, intolerance, and discrimination through education and litigation. Its programs include Teaching Tolerance and the Intelligence Project, which incorporates Klanwatch and the Militia Task Force.

Voters Telecommunications Watch (VTW)
233 Court St., Suite 2, Brooklyn, NY 11201
(718) 596-2851
e-mail: vtw@vtw.org • website: www.vtw.org

VTW is a coalition of civil liberties organizations that actively participates in the democratic and legislative processes to promote civil liberties for telecommunications users. It recommends legislation, monitors the positions and voting records of elected officials, and informs and alerts the public on relevant issues. VTW publishes *VTW-Announce*, a weekly online newsletter that chronicles federal legislation affecting telecommunications and civil liberties.

Bibliography of Books

Janet Abbate — *Inventing the Internet*. Cambridge, MA: MIT Press, 1999.

David Brown — *Cybertrends: Chaos, Power, and Accountability in the Information Age*. New York: Viking, 1997.

Andrew Calcutt — *White Noise: An A–Z of the Contradictions in Cyberculture*. New York: St. Martin's Press, 1999.

Jim Davis, Thomas Hirschl, and Michael Stack — *Cutting Edge: Technology, Information, Capitalism, and Social Revolution*. New York: Verso Books, 1998.

Michael L. Dertouzos — *What Will Be: How the New World of Information Will Change Our Lives*. San Francisco: HarperEdge, 1997.

Stephen Doheny-Farina — *The Wired Neighborhood*. New Haven, CT: Yale University Press, 1996.

James A. Dorn, ed. — *How the Internet Will Change the Economy*. Washington, DC: Cato Institute, 1999.

Esther Dyson — *Release 2.0: A Design for Living in the Digital Age*. New York: Broadway Books, 1997.

Bill Gates — *The Road Ahead*. New York: Penguin, 1996.

Paul Gilster — *Digital Literacy*. New York: John Wiley and Sons, 1997.

Mike Godwin — *Cyber Rights: Defending Free Speech in the Digital Age*. New York: Random House, 1998.

David N. Greenfield — *Virtual Addiction: Help for Netheads, Cyber Freaks, and Those Who Love Them*. Oakland, CA: New Harbinger, 1999.

Douglas Groothuis — *The Soul in Cyberspace*. Grand Rapids, MI: Baker Book House, 1999.

Jon Katz — *Media Rants: Postpolitics in the Digital Nation*. San Francisco: Hardwired, 1997.

Peter Ludlow, ed. — *High Noon on the Electronic Frontier: Conceptual Issues in Cyberspace*. Cambridge, MA: MIT Press, 1996.

William J. Mitchell — *City of Bits: Space, Place, and the Infobahn*. Cambridge, MA: MIT Press, 1996.

William J. Mitchell — *E-Topia*. Cambridge, MA: MIT Press, 2000.

Christos J.P. Moschovitis — *History of the Internet: A Chronology, 1843 to the Present*. Santa Barbara, CA: ABC-CLIO, 1999.

John Naughton	*A Brief History of the Future: Origins of the Internet*. New York: Overlook Press, 2000.
Charles Platt	*Anarchy Online*. New York: HarperPrism, 1996.
Gregory J.E. Rawlins	*Moths to the Flame: The Seduction of Computer Technology*. Cambridge, MA: MIT Press, 1996.
Jeremy Rifkin	*The Age of Access: The New Culture of Hypercapitalism Where All Life Is a Paid-For Experience*. New York: Putnam, 2000.
Gene I. Rochlin	*Trapped in the Net: The Unanticipated Consequences of Computerization*. New Jersey: Princeton University Press, 1998.
Herbert Schiller	*Information Inequality: The Deepening Social Crisis in America*. New York: Routledge, 1996.
Andrew L. Shapiro	*Control Revolution: How the Internet Is Putting Individuals in Charge and Changing the World as We Know It*. New York: Public Affairs, 2000.
David Shenk	*Data Smog*. San Francisco: HarperEdge, 1997.
Marc Smith and Peter Kollack, eds.	*Communities in Cyberspace*. New York: Routledge, 1998.
Clifford Stoll	*High Tech Heretic: Reflections of a Computer Contrarian*. New York: Anchor Press, 2000.
Clifford Stoll	*Silicon Snake Oil: Second Thoughts on the Information Highway*. New York: Anchor Press, 1996.
Chris Toulouse and Timothy W. Luke, eds.	*The Politics of Cyberspace: A New Political Science Reader*. New York: Routledge, 1998.
Gary Young, ed.	*The Internet*. New York: H.W. Wilson, 1998.
Kimberly S. Young	*Caught in the Net: How to Recognize the Signs of Internet Addiction—And a Winning Strategy for Recovery*. John Wiley and Sons, 1998.
Jonathan Wallace and Mark Mangan	*Sex, Laws, and Cyberspace*. New York: Owl Books, 1997.
Patricia M. Wallace	*The Psychology of the Internet*. New York: Cambridge University Press, 1999.
David B. Whittle	*Cyberspace: The Human Dimension*. New York: W.H. Freeman, 1997.
Jeff Zaleski	*The Soul of Cyberspace: How New Technology Is Changing Our Spiritual Lives*. San Francisco: HarperEdge, 1998.

Index

Irving, Larry, 40

Jackson, Jesse, 39, 44
Janklow, William, 142
Johnson, David, 110
Journal of the American Medical Association (JAMA), 106
Joy, Bill, 170, 171

Kaczmarczyk, Steven, 94
Kairys, Stepas, 193
Kaiser Family Foundation, 34
Karman, Jay, 51
Keating, Raymond J., 143
Kedrosky, Paul, 188
Kincaid, James R., 68
Klanwatch Project, 28
Koop, C. Everett, 99
Kraft, Paul, 96
Kushner, David, 88

Lamberg, Lynne, 98
LaRue, Melody, 47
laws
  copyright, 153–54
  against Internet pornography, should be enforced, 122–28
    con, 129–35
  privacy
    are necessary, 111–15
      con, 116–21
    economics of, 118–20
  regulating anonymity of Internet users, 110
  see also names of individual laws
Levin, Gerald, 178
Litt, Robert, 58
Livdahl, Todd, 190
Lochhead, Chris, 187
Los Angeles Times (newspaper), 15
Lukas, Aaron, 145
Lundgren, Sean, 190

Madara, Ed, 99
Madison, James, 134
Manning, David, 100
Marcus, Brian, 46, 49, 51
Martine, Cathy-Ann, 193
Maxwell, Bruce, 194
MayberryUSA, 133
McChesney, Robert, 175
McCormick, Brian, 17
McCullagh, Declan, 56, 116
McMartin Preschool case, 72
"media viruses," 27–28
medical information
  on Internet

criteria for evaluating, 106
  may be unreliable, 103–107
Mennahum, David, 13
Mfume, Kweisi, 39
Microsoft Internet Explorer, 14, 181
  filtering capabilities of, 134
Miller, Greg, 119
Miller v. California, 125
Mitchell, Daniel, 145
Mitchell, William J., 27
Mossberg, Walter, 148
Muri, Scott, 91
music
  distribution over Internet should be regulated, 147–50
    con, 151–55
  racist, on Internet, 53

Napster, 148–49
National Center for Missing and Exploited Children, 70
Naughton, Patrick, 69, 73
Neff, Raymond, 172
Netscape Navigator Web browser, 14
  filtering capabilities of, 134
Net2Phone, 195, 197
New Century Network, 177
newsgroups, 14
New York Times (newspaper), 178
Nie, Norman, 19
Norman, Michael Van, 196

Oklahoma City bombing, 26
  Internet communication on, 167
Operation Innocent Images Task Force, 59, 69, 72
Owens, Bill, 114

Parent's Guide to Internet Safety, A (FBI), 130
Pathfinder, 177
Patrick, John, 171, 173, 174
pedophilia
  is serious problem on the Internet, 59–67
    con, 68–75
  as sexual orientation, 64–65
Pew Research Center for the People and the Press, 15
Phelps, Fred, 48
"Phineas Priests," 49
Pierce, William, 53
Pitofsky, Robert, 117
Platt, Charles, 54
pornography
  government should not regulate, 129–35